TOP 10
COSTA RICA
ITINERARIES

TOP 10 COSTA RICA ITINERARIES

MATTHEW HOUDE

JENNIFER TURNBULL

TRAVELOGUE ADVENTURES

DISCLAIMER

This book is intended to provide helpful and informative material on the subjects addressed herein. Although the information provided was accurate as of publication, things can change quickly in Costa Rica so it's best to check schedules, prices, and rates before traveling to obtain the most current information. The authors have taken all reasonable care in preparing this book, but they make no warranty about its accuracy or completeness and, to the maximum extent permitted, disclaim all liability arising from its use.

CONTENTS

ITINERARIES

Contents

Contents

Contents

ACTIVITIES GUIDE

Contents

INTRODUCTION

Costa Rica is a destination full of surprises. When we first began visiting this small Central American country nearly ten years ago, we were in awe of our surroundings. Dramatic landscapes of lush rainforest, exotic birds and animals, beautiful beaches, and a culture of friendly people. Every year we returned, escaping the frigid northeastern United States, and every year, Costa Rica showed us something new and exciting. In 2012, we published a travelogue about one of those whimsical visits called *Two Weeks in Costa Rica*. Writing that book only solidified our love for the country, and soon, visiting just once a year wasn't enough.

In 2013, we moved to Costa Rica full time and began slow traveling the country, spending weeks or sometimes months in each place. From the Pacific to the Caribbean, we have explored Costa Rica's booming resort towns, quaint fishing villages, and everything in between. We've met rural coffee farmers, climbed active volcanos, and dined with Ticos who have helped us along the way. We've pushed ourselves to see and do things we never would have done before, and in doing so, have gained invaluable insight into the country.

The purpose of this book is to share some of these insights in a simple, straightforward way. Simply pick one of the ten itineraries based on your interests to discover where to visit in one or two weeks. Whether you're visiting Costa Rica to see wildlife or for surfing, adventure, a family getaway, eco-trekking, an authentic experience, or just to relax on the beach, there is an itinerary for you. And for those looking for the best all-around experience, our

Best of Costa Rica itinerary showcases some of the country's top destinations and sights.

Through any one of the itineraries, you can plan the framework for your entire trip. Each one pinpoints destinations and provides a general overview so that you know what to expect. You'll get a feel for each town, its layout, landscape, and available amenities. While we do not provide specific hotel and restaurant recommendations in order to keep this book focused and streamlined, we explain the types of lodging and restaurants that are available in each town. We also highlight the must-see activities and attractions based on your interests. Finally, each itinerary recommends the best order for your travels and shows you how to get from place to place.

Throughout the text, you will see our insider tips. These tips include everything from essential information on transportation, like if a four-wheel-drive vehicle is needed, to guidance on a particular activity or sight. To further help you plan, we provide additional detail on certain topics in resource guides at the end of the book. The Transportation Guide summarizes the best transportation options for each itinerary and includes estimated travel times whether you're driving, taking a shuttle van, or flying. We also provide estimated costs and special notes when necessary. The Activities Guide gives more information for the activities recommended, like hours of operation, website links, price, etc.

A note on our recommendations: You'll notice that we sometimes provide the names of specific tour operators. Know that we gain nothing financially from doing so. We've based all our recommendations on our own experiences and what we have learned from other locals or travelers. We only provide this information to ease the planning process and point you in the right direction where tours are difficult to find or completely unique.

ADDITIONAL HELP AND
OUR TRAVEL FORUM

Hopefully one of these itineraries is the perfect fit and all you have left to do is pick out hotels and arrange transportation. If you do find yourself needing more help, a good place to start is our website, www.twoweeksincostarica.com. We are constantly adding new information about destinations, activities, and accommodations to our site. If something isn't covered, we also have a travel forum where you can ask us your questions directly: www.twoweeksincostarica.com/forum.

1

BEST OF COSTA RICA

Though small in size, Costa Rica is incredibly diverse. With two oceans and four mountain ranges, cool cloud forest and balmy tropical rainforest, it boasts more attractions than you could ever see in just one or two weeks. Our Best of Costa Rica itinerary has been carefully designed to give you a feel for the entire country and show you the must-see attractions, while still ensuring a relaxing getaway. From the jungle-backed beaches of the central Pacific coast, to the volcanos and misty cloud forests of the mountains, to the wild Osa Peninsula, you'll experience the very best of Costa Rica. And unlike the rest of this book, which is aimed toward specific types of travel, this itinerary will appeal to anyone regardless of age, interests, or travel style.

One Week Itinerary: La Fortuna (3 days) to Manuel Antonio (4 days). Recommended Airport: SJO. View transportation options for this itinerary on p. 126.

Two Week Itinerary: La Fortuna (3 days) to Monteverde (3 days) to Manuel Antonio (4 days) to Drake Bay (4 days). Recommended Airport: SJO. View transportation options for this itinerary on p. 127.

La Fortuna

One Week Itinerary: La Fortuna – Days 1-3

Two Week Itinerary: La Fortuna – Days 1-3

You'll notice that La Fortuna appears in many of the itineraries in this book. That's not by chance. With an array of tourist amenities, one of the top attractions in the country, and convenience to international airports, La Fortuna is a premier destination in Costa Rica. Though this mountain gem is undoubtedly growing in popularity, it still has a small-town feel and is the perfect place to begin your tropical getaway.

Nestled in the hills in northwestern Costa Rica about 3-4 hours from San José, La Fortuna is a former farming town located near the base of Arenal Volcano. Much of the area's businesses are concentrated in the vibrant downtown, but many travelers prefer to stay in the jungle surrounds where it is quieter and more secluded. Lodging ranges from world-renowned five-star resorts and fully equipped vacation rentals to eco-lodges, hotels, and rustic bungalows.

Tip: One of the biggest complaints travelers to the Arenal area have is feeling stuck at the resort. Many of the popular hotels are located more remotely on the road to Lake Arenal, quite far from attractions and amenities. Cab fares can get expensive so you may want to consider renting a car if you stay outside the downtown.

The Highlight

From La Fortuna, you can do just about all the quintessential Costa Rica adventure activities. But the biggest attraction you won't find anywhere else is the giant cone-shaped volcano. Standing at 1,630 meters (5,347 feet) tall, Arenal Volcano put La Fortuna on the map with its frequent activity. For over 40 years, Arenal erupted almost every day, leaving visitors in awe of its lava flows, which glowed bright orange at night. Although today it is no longer erupting, Arenal still remains an amazing sight and can be seen for miles around on a clear day.

The mighty Arenal Volcano

To get a closer look, head to the area's many hiking trails. **Arenal Volcano National Park** (p. 162) and **Arenal 1968** (p. 162) offer easy-to-moderately difficult walking trails, which pass through former lava fields from the last big eruption in the late sixties. The **Arenal Observatory** (p. 162) is also an excellent choice for exploring the volcano. This lodge has a network of trails of different lengths and levels of difficulty, making it good for people of all fitness levels and children. It also has a viewing platform for people with limited mobility, and an on-site restaurant to grab a bite to eat after you've worked up an appetite.

Other Activities and Attractions

La Fortuna has upwards of 100 activities and attractions, more than you could ever do in just one vacation. To get the most out of your stay, focus on the area's most unique sights. Something that you don't want to miss is the **hot springs** (p. 162), which are naturally heated by the volcano's thermal energy. Many hotels have spring-fed pools on site, but if yours doesn't, resort day passes allow you to soak in mineral-rich pools surrounded by lush gardens. Alternatively, you can go the more rustic route and join the locals for a warm soak in the river near the Tabacon Resort for free.

Another must-see is **La Fortuna Waterfall** (p. 163), which cascades 70 meters (230 feet) into a teal-colored pool. This is a very powerful waterfall that gushes even during the dry season. You can access it by horseback tour, but many people prefer to go on their own via the visitors center. Be prepared for a hike down 500 steep, but well maintained, steps and take a bathing suit to splash along the edge of the natural pool.

For a little excitement, take a **white-water rafting tour** (p. 164) through Costa Rica's dense jungle. The La Fortuna area has several swift-moving rivers to choose from of varying levels of difficulty. The Balsa River is the closest to town and features rapids for all levels, from easy level II runs all the way up to expert class V. Farther to the east, the Toro River has a good mixture of fun and thrill with class III to IV white water, while the Sarapiquí River has more mellow waters, which range from II to III.

If you have more time, other popular activities include mountain biking around Lake Arenal, exploring the rainforest canopy at the **Arenal Hanging Bridges** (p. 163), zip lining, kayaking, spelunking through the **Venado Bat Caves** (p. 164), a night tour to see frogs, snakes, and other nocturnal creatures, and visiting the **Proyecto Asis Wildlife Center** (p. 163) to see toucans, monkeys, sloths, and more.

Tip: Keep in mind that some activities are weather dependent (e.g., Arenal Volcano is sometimes enshrouded in clouds and not visible, especially in the rainier months of July through November). You may want to allow for flexibility in your itinerary and wait to book some of your activities when you arrive.

Monteverde

One Week Itinerary: Skip Monteverde. Go directly to Manuel Antonio.

Two Week Itinerary: Monteverde – Days 4-6

If you have two weeks to spend in Costa Rica, you don't want to miss the cloud forest. After your first stop in La Fortuna, head to Monteverde for a few nights before making your way south to Manuel Antonio.

Monteverde is located a few hours from La Fortuna along an infamously bumpy dirt road. Although it doesn't take too long to get there, you'll feel like you're in another world. Due to its high elevation and location at the Continental Divide, Monteverde is often covered in misty clouds, which come and go with the shifting winds. The trees and plants are laden with moss because of the moisture, and temperatures are a lot cooler (averaging 19°C/66°F).

The entire area is commonly called Monteverde (Green Mountain) but actually encompasses two separate towns. Santa Elena is the first you'll come to and is home to many of the area hotels and restaurants. Continuing on, you'll enter Monteverde, which is more spread out, with businesses located along the main road and smaller offshoots.

Despite being a major tourist destination, Monteverde isn't too developed and still has a small-town charm. Most of the hotels are eco-lodges, which fit nicely into the natural surroundings. You'll find everything from over-the-top luxury treehouses to simple, rustic cabins, almost always with great views of the verdant hills.

Tip: The drive from La Fortuna to Monteverde requires four-wheel drive. After you pass the small city of Tilarán, the road turns to rough dirt. If you're at all nervous, leave the driving to someone else and take the Jeep-Boat-Jeep, a shuttle service from La Fortuna, which includes a boat transfer across Lake Arenal. See the Transportation Guide (p. 127) for more information.

The Highlight

The highlight of Monteverde is of course the cloud forest, which can be explored in many different ways. For hanging bridges, head to **Selvatura** (p. 167) or **Sky Adventures** (p. 167). They have the best facilities for hanging bridges in the country, with nice walking trails and a sequence of safe bridges that will get you up at canopy level, making it a lot easier to spot wildlife. If you're traveling with someone with limited mobility, you may also want to check out the tram at Sky Adventures, one of the few attractions in Costa Rica that are wheelchair accessible.

If you would prefer to explore the area's misty forests on day hikes, there are several reserves. The most popular is the **Monteverde Cloud Forest Reserve** (p. 167), which has trails for all levels and one hanging bridge. The Monteverde Reserve can get busy during the high season, so if you'd rather avoid the crowds, head to either **Curi Cancha** (p. 166) or the higher elevation **Santa Elena Cloud Forest Reserve** (p. 167). Both have similar trails and habitat to the Monteverde Reserve but are much less busy.

Tip: To see the most wildlife, hire a guide. Monteverde is one of the most biologically rich areas of Costa Rica, but it can be difficult to spot birds and animals due to the thick forest and hazy cloud cover. Guides know where to look and will spot things you would have otherwise missed without their trained eye.

Finally, **zip lining** (p. 168) is the most exciting way to experience the cloud forest. Zip lining in Costa Rica began in Monteverde, and while there are several companies now offering tours, the experience is still the same. You'll speed above the canopy to see breathtaking jungle views and maybe even Arenal Volcano and the Pacific Ocean in the distance.

Other Activities and Attractions

The **Hummingbird Gallery** (p. 167) near the Monteverde Cloud Forest Reserve is a quick stop that you won't regret. Outside the small gift shop are feeders, which attract dozens of different hummingbird species. These tiny birds will practically fly into you as they speed from feeder to feeder, allowing you to see them close up. Be sure to take your camera.

Another popular activity, which will have you buzzing around yourself, is a coffee tour. Due to its high altitude, this region of Costa Rica has ideal conditions for growing coffee, and small farms dot the steep hills outside town. To learn more about these famous Arabica beans and the work that goes into each cup, take a tour with **El Trapiche** (p. 166), **Don Juan** (p. 166), **El Cafetal** (p. 166), or one of the many other regional growers.

Finally, when in Monteverde, a trip to the **Monteverde Cheese Factory** (p. 167) to sample *queso* or grab an ice cream is also mandatory. Though now a modern factory, the company was started by Quakers who founded the area's first dairy farms in the 1950s. If you still haven't had your fill of fun, other activities in the area include horseback riding, the **Serpentarium** (p. 167), the **Bat Jungle** (p. 166), canyoning (waterfall rappelling), four-wheeling, and perusing the many shops and art galleries around town.

Manuel Antonio

One Week Itinerary: Manuel Antonio – Days 4-7

Two Week Itinerary: Manuel Antonio – Days 7-10

Once you've explored the forests and volcanos of the mountains, take in the warm, salty air of the central Pacific coast. Located on a point about 4-5 hours from La Fortuna or 3-4 hours from Monteverde, Manuel Antonio is a favorite beach town with all the amenities. Although geographically small in size, there is a lot squeezed into this small community. Along the one main road, which begins in the port of Quepos and ends 7 km (4.3 miles) later at the beach, is an abundance of hotels, restaurants, and shops. Though Manuel Antonio is indeed developed, complete with luxury resorts, infinity pools, and fine dining, it still brims with lush rainforest and wildlife.

Tip: This is another destination where hotel location matters. The top of the hill (near the Barba Roja restaurant) has the best ocean views and easy access to restaurants and supermarkets. The drawback is that you'll be farther from the beach. To be a short walk to the beach and Manuel Antonio National Park, stay near the bottom of the hill on the southern end of town.

The Highlight

The highlight of Manuel Antonio is its pristine beaches. The main beach, Playa Espadilla, and several smaller beaches line the rainforest-fringed coastline and are the focal point of the entire community.

The long gray sand Playa Espadilla is the most popular beach in town and fills up quickly with vacationers looking to swim, surf, jet ski, jog, or just relax from the comfort of a beach chair. It can get busy and during holidays is usually a patchwork of beach umbrellas, but you can almost always find seclusion at the northern end.

The southern end of Playa Espadilla

Playa Espadilla can have strong riptides, so for calmer water, head to **Manuel Antonio National Park** (p. 165). Playa Manuel Antonio is the first beach you'll come to in the park and is a popular spot to spend the day. This horseshoe-shaped cove has calm water for swimming, almond trees for lounging, and rocks for snorkeling. Playa Manuel Antonio tends to be the busiest inside the park, so for more seclusion, keep walking to Playa Espadilla Sur just past the first beach.

A favorite beach among the locals is **Playa Biesanz**. This sheltered cove with serene aquamarine water is a hidden gem in Manuel Antonio, located a short walk through the woods off the road going to the Parador Resort and Spa. Playa Biesanz is not marked so refer to the Activities Guide (p. 165) for guidance on getting there.

Other Activities and Attractions

Aside from the beaches, Manuel Antonio is also famed for its wildlife and you don't have to go far to find it. Manuel Antonio National Park, located at the end of the road in town, is Costa Rica's smallest park at about 20 sq km (8 sq miles), yet is by far the most popular. The reason for its broad appeal is those beautiful beaches we mention above, the trail system which is good for all levels, and how easy it is to spot wildlife.

Before you start envisioning a private nature oasis full of monkeys, exotic birds, and sloths (all which can be spotted), know that the park can get very busy, and during peak seasons can feel a bit like Disneyland. The best way to avoid the crowds is to arrive early when the park opens (7:00 a.m.) and stick to the side trails, which tend to be less busy. *Closed Mondays during the low season (July 1 – Nov. 30).*

A quieter option for wildlife viewing just 30 minutes north of Manuel Antonio is the **Rainmaker Conservation Project** (p. 165). This 607 hectare (1,500 acre) reserve protects a giant parcel of primary rainforest, which was almost turned into a lumber yard. Along the reserve's 2.5 km (1.5 miles) of trails, you can see animals like poison dart frogs, blue morpho butterflies, snakes, lizards, toucans, and lots of interesting insects. Rainmaker's trail system is moderately difficult with some steep areas, slippery spots, and a series of hanging bridges and platforms that are not for the faint of heart. Part of the trail follows a river and waterfall where you can cool off with a swim.

Other great ways to spot wildlife near Manuel Antonio are on a kayak or boat tour through the mangroves of **Isla Damas** (p. 164), just north of Manuel Antonio, or by visiting the wildlife sanctuary and Sloth Institute at **Kids Saving the Rainforest** (p. 164).

Like La Fortuna, the possibilities for tours are almost

endless in Manuel Antonio. Popular ways to explore the ocean are surfing, stand-up paddleboarding, a catamaran tour, sportfishing, or if you want some adventure, parasailing or jet skiing. To take adventure to the extreme, check out the Superman, one of Costa Rica's longest zip lines, go white-water rafting on the Savegre or Naranjo Rivers, or try canyoning (waterfall rappelling). Other activities in the area include a tour of the **Rainforest Spices farm** (p. 165), horseback riding, and ATV tours.

Drake Bay

One Week Itinerary: Omitted. Trip ends in Manuel Antonio.

Two Week Itinerary: Drake Bay – Days 11-14

For the final leg of your two-week vacation, head south from Manuel Antonio to the rugged Osa Peninsula. Brimming with virgin tropical rainforest, this undeveloped area is the perfect place to just relax and unwind in beautiful natural surroundings. From the riverside town of Sierpe (2 hours from Manuel Antonio), you'll take a short boat ride through the mangroves to reach Drake Bay on the southern Pacific coast. Only accessible by boat or small plane, this isolated village set in the middle of the jungle will give you a true taste of Costa Rica's wild side.

Tips: Be sure to take a flashlight. Drake didn't get electricity until 2004, and lighting is used much less than what you're probably used to. Also be sure to stock up on cash in advance as there are no ATMs.

Despite its remoteness, Drake Bay offers many conveniences for travelers. Accommodations range from modern bungalows and B&Bs to family-run cabins and beachside tent camps. When considering hotels, keep in mind that many include meals, transfers, and tours in the nightly rate.

Transportation Tips: Although it is possible to drive to Drake Bay, it is not recommended. The roads are rough dirt and there are multiple river crossings best forded by only the most experienced locals. You won't need a car once you arrive in Drake Bay anyway, as most people get around on foot. After your time in Drake, you can take a small plane back to San José to save time. Refer to our Transportation Guide (p. 127) for more information.

The Highlight

The highlight of Drake Bay is its wild jungle. While you'll be surrounded by rainforest during your entire stay in Drake Bay, for the full experience, visit **Corcovado National Park** (p. 159). This massive swath of lowland rainforest covers much of the Osa Peninsula. It is so remote that you can't access most of it, but there is a network of trails ready to be explored.

The best way to access the park's trails from Drake Bay is to take a boat to either San Pedrillo or Sirena Ranger Stations. On a day trip or overnight stay, a guide will lead you on a hike and show you some of Corcovado's amazing wildlife. Considered to be one of the most biologically diverse places on earth, Corcovado is home to rare creatures like the Baird's tapir, white-lipped peccaries, collared anteaters, Scarlet Macaw parrots, fer de lance snakes, all four types of monkeys that live in Costa Rica, and even big cats like pumas and jaguars. Many travelers say that their visit to Corcovado was the most memorable part of their entire trip. *Note: All visits to Corcovado must be arranged through a registered guide (available through tour operators in Drake Bay). See the Activities Guide (p. 159) for more information.*

Other Activities and Attractions

Another way to experience the amazing nature of Drake Bay is to take a snorkel or dive tour. Located just 16 km (10 miles) off the coast, **Caño Island** (p. 159) offers some of the clearest water in Costa Rica. Along the reefs, you may see needlefish, parrotfish, puffers, rays, sea turtles, and whitetip reef sharks. Dolphins and migrating whales also inhabit Caño's marine-rich waters, and tours to spot them are also available.

Another great activity that is especially popular with kids is a **night walk** (p. 160). On a night-time forest walk with a headlamp to light your way, you'll get to learn more about the creatures that only come out after dark like tree frogs, scorpions, snakes, and other creepy crawlies.

Although you need a guide to hike in Corcovado National Park, you won't need one to visit Playa San Josecito. This beach is accessible by following the long coastal path south of town that eventually leads to Corcovado. Along the remote trail, you'll pass many desolate, rock-flanked beaches and are likely to see some of the same wildlife you'd see in the park. Plan for an entire day to get to beach and back and take plenty of water as it can be extremely hot.

Other activities in Drake Bay include a night swim to see glowing blue bioluminescent plankton, kayaking, horseback riding, sportfishing, and bird-watching.

2

AUTHENTIC COSTA RICA

Costa Rica is quickly becoming a top destination in Latin America, but there are still plenty of off-the-beaten-path places where you can experience the real Costa Rica. In this itinerary, we guide you through destinations rich in history, culture, and tradition, all while highlighting the country's famed natural attractions. From the Caribbean coast where Columbus first landed, to the Central Valley where most of the population lives and works, you will meet the faces of this small Central American nation and get a feel for everyday Tico life. For those with more time, a two-week itinerary delves deeper into the culture, taking you to a mountain town famous for pre-Columbian ruins and the dry northwestern plains where cowboys still ride horses alongside modern highways.

One Week Itinerary: Cahuita (4 days) to Grecia/Atenas (3 days). Recommended Airport: SJO. View transportation options for this itinerary on p. 129.

Two Week Itinerary: Cahuita (4 days) to Turrialba (3 days) to Grecia/Atenas (4 days) to Liberia/Guanacaste Province (3 days). Recommended Airport: SJO. View transportation options for this itinerary on p. 130.

Cahuita

One Week Itinerary: Cahuita – Days 1-4

Two Week Itinerary: Cahuita – Days 1-4

The first stop on your authentic trek through Costa Rica is the Caribbean coast. Christopher Columbus first landed on the shores of Limón in 1502, hoping to find riches, but saw only swampy jungle and a few indigenous tribes. It wouldn't be until hundreds of years later that growth would finally come. The construction of the railroad and port of Limón in the late 1800s, as well as the explosion of the coffee and banana trades, brought droves of people from the West Indies looking for work. Over time, their Afro-Caribbean traditions mixed with existing indigenous and Spanish cultures to create a Caribbean-island feel on Costa Rica's east coast. Cahuita, just south of Limón, is a great place to experience this unique regional culture.

Cahuita is a peaceful coastal village about 3-4 hours from San José with brightly painted wooden buildings, dusty dirt roads, lush jungle, and many secluded beaches. You won't find any fancy resorts in this quaint town, but there are a good selection of smaller lodges, inns, and seaside bungalows. Family-run restaurants are spread out along the main drags and offer traditional Caribbean cuisine with flavors of coconut, lime, and chilies.

The Highlight

The highlight of Cahuita is the Afro-Caribbean culture. Although a lot has changed since immigrants and former slaves came to help build a railroad to San José, many traditions remain. Calypso and reggae bands play in local bars, coconut rice is served with spicy sauces, and some old-timers still speak an English-based Creole called Mekatelyu. Exploring the town is as much about exploring the people who live in it. In the streets, you will meet locals riding bicycles, and along the beaches you will find them launching their colorful boats or hand-line fishing from shore.

Two major events in the area celebrate the Afro-Caribbean heritage. Carnival in Limón is held in October and features elaborate parades, live music, and street vendors. In late August, there is also the Festival Flores de la Diáspora Africana, which has events that spread from the cinemas and theaters of San José to the streets and plazas of Puerto Viejo de Talamanca to the south.

Other Activities and Attractions

In addition to the Afro-Caribbean culture, the area is home to several indigenous communities who have lived on the Caribbean slope for centuries. Day trips and overnight stays with groups like the Bribri are a great way to see how Costa Rica's indigenous have adapted to the modern world, all while keeping their traditions alive. On one of these tours, you will be invited into traditional thatched roof homes to learn about rituals and farming practices that have been passed down for generations. Cacao is one of the Bribri's most interesting crops and is still used today in sacred ceremonies. Tours can be arranged through **ATEC** (p. 155), the local community tourism organization.

Even if you don't visit one of the indigenous communities, it is worth taking a chocolate tour to learn about cacao's cultural significance in Costa Rica. **Caribeans** (p. 170) is about 20 minutes away in Puerto Viejo and offers an interactive and informative tour. You will walk the cacao forest and see how artisanal chocolate is made bean to bar using fair trade ingredients from indigenous groups and local farmers. Don't miss a stop in their tasting room. Another great option closer to Cahuita is **Cacao Trails** (p. 156), a combination chocolate museum and factory, botanical garden, and farm. Cacao Trails offers a range of tours from a 45 minute chocolate tour if you're short on time to a longer in-depth tour of the entire property.

A cacao pod next to the final product, rich dark chocolate

Other activities in the area include a hike through **Cahuita National Park** (p. 156) to spot wildlife like monkeys, sloths, and birds, or a snorkel tour around Cahuita's pristine coral reefs to see colorful fish. There are also two highly recommended refuges close by, which rescue and rehabilitate local wildlife, the **Sloth Sanctuary** (p. 156) and **Tree of Life Wildlife Rescue Center & Botanical Gardens** (p. 156).

Turrialba

One Week Itinerary: Skip Turrialba and go directly to Grecia/Atenas.

Two Week Itinerary: Turrialba – Days 5-7

For the two-week vacationer, on your way to Grecia or Atenas from Cahuita, stop for a few days in the small city of Turrialba about 2.5 hours away. Turrialba sits low in a valley and has a busy downtown, which serves as the hub for smaller communities that stretch into the hills. The main area of town has a few simple hotels, but most guests choose to catch the lofty views from lodges and bed and breakfasts in the surrounding mountains.

In Turrialba, you will get to witness the daily happenings of a typical Costa Rican city, all while absorbing some of its history, which dates back hundreds and even thousands of years. Turrialba is located along the original route to the Caribbean coast, which first connected the capital of San José to Limón. The old train tracks are still visible along the busy streets and an original steam engine from the 1800s is displayed at the local university. Although a new highway to the Caribbean coast bypasses this historic town, there is nonetheless a lot of history and culture to absorb.

The Highlight

The authentic highlight of Turrialba is the **Guayabo National Monument** (p. 173). These archeological ruins set high atop a nearby mountain are considered one of Costa Rica's most important historic sights. Although not nearly as impressive as other well-known ruins like the Yucatán in Mexico or Tikal in Guatemala, they still provide an interesting glimpse into the past.

Thought to have been inhabited from 1000 BC until AD 1400, the remains of this mysterious village are still turning up clues about how people lived on the isthmus before the arrival of Europeans. Walking along the trails, you will be able to see the mossy stone mounds and weathered steps, which were once foundations for impressive thatched roof homes and places of worship. Additionally, an aqueduct system still collects pure water from a mountain stream and an excavated stone road shows how this ancient community was once connected.

From a viewpoint, you can start to imagine what this town might have looked like in its prime. Along the nicely maintained nature trails are also a few tombs and petroglyphs. **Tip:** To get the most out of your visit, hire a guide. Guides are available for a small fee and are very knowledgeable about the monument's artifacts. For more information on arranging a guide, see the Activities Guide (p. 173).

Other Activities and Attractions

Besides Guayabo, Turrialba has many more things for which it is known. Around the base of the nearby Turrialba Volcano, some impressive farming takes place. Nearly 275 dairy farms and 150 small cheese plants produce one of the country's most popular dairy products, Turrialba cheese. A visit to a local dairy farm in the village of Santa Cruz de Turrialba, like **La Finca Florita** (p. 173), can offer you a taste of this mild *queso*, all while showing you how it has been made for nearly 150 years.

Also nearby is **CATIE** (Centro Agronómico Tropical de Investigación y Enseñanza) (p. 173). This agricultural research center near the university downtown has a beautiful and biologically rich property where you can take an informative tour to learn about the most cutting edge farming and conservation practices involving coffee, chocolate, dairy, and tropical plants.

While Turrialba offers much insight into Costa Rica's history and traditions, it is best known in the travel world for its unparalleled **white-water rafting** (p. 174). The Pacuare River provides consistently challenging rapids and a chance to float through some of the country's most scenic jungle. For those seeking a mellower ride, the Pejibaye River offers class II and III rapids as well (see chapter on Adventure, p. 37, for more information).

On your way back to the Central Valley, more sights include the stunning green crater lake at **Irazú Volcano**

(p. 173) (best viewed on sunny days) as well as a stop in Cartago. Cartago was Costa Rica's first capital city and it is worth taking a few minutes to see the country's most revered religious site, Basilica de Nuestra Señora de los Angeles (Basilica of Our Lady of the Angels) (1635), and the nearby Las Ruinas de la Parroquia (the Ruins of the Parish) (1575), which today functions as a park.

Grecia/Atenas

One Week Itinerary: Grecia/Atenas – Days 5-7

Two Week Itinerary: Grecia/Atenas – Days 8-11

For a true sense of local life in Costa Rica, head to the mountains of the Central Valley (around 3 hours from Turrialba; 4-5 hours from Cahuita) for a few days. This region is where most Costa Ricans live and work and is also where the country's most renowned cultural sights can be found.

To experience the flavor of the Central Valley while escaping the hustle and bustle of the capital city of San José, stay in the suburban towns of Grecia or Atenas. From either locale, you can easily explore the area on day trips and then retreat to the tranquil hills at night. Of the two, Grecia is the largest and has a bustling downtown centered on a historic church and park. Atenas, slightly farther west of San José, also has a concentrated downtown but is smaller and less busy. Both offer charming bed-and-breakfast-style lodging, set among fields of coffee and sugarcane.

The Highlight

The highlight of your time in the Central Valley is a

traditional coffee tour. Farming, especially coffee farming, has played a major role in shaping the country's infrastructure and economy over the last 150 plus years. Today, coffee provides a livelihood for countless Costa Rican families who rely on the region's rich volcanic soil, consistent rainfall, and moderate temperatures to grow some of the finest coffee cherries in the world.

Unlike much of Central America, Costa Rican coffee is produced mostly on a small scale by family-owned growers. For a glimpse into Costa Rica's coffee culture, visit one of the thousands of these small growers during your time in the Central Valley. A couple of excellent tours are **El Toledo** (p. 156) in Atenas and **Espíritu Santo** (p. 157) in Naranjo, both of which offer insight into the everyday struggles and successes of today's proud producers.

Other Activities and Attractions

Once you've seen how coffee is grown, find out how it was transported prior to today's modern technology. In the town of Sarchí near Grecia, you can watch local artisans fabricate and hand paint *carretas* (oxcarts), which were once used to haul coffee all the way to the coast.

Around Grecia, visit the historic metal church near the central park, which stands out with its bright red metal walls, or stroll through the Central Market and sit down for a *casado* (traditional plate of rice and beans with meat or fish). If you happen to be visiting on a Friday or Saturday, wander around the *feria* (farmers market) to see locals in their daily lives, buying produce, meats, cheeses, and other goodies.

Also near Grecia are the little-known **Los Chorros Waterfalls** (p. 157). Most often visited by locals, Los Chorros are a set of two waterfalls south of town. The first falls (around 40 meters or 130 feet tall) are the easiest to get to and are accessible from a parking area via a

15 minute walk through the woods. Be sure to take your suit for swimming. Los Chorros are not marked so refer to the Activities Guide (p. 157) for directions.

Another great way to learn about Costa Rica's history and culture is by visiting downtown San José. For two sights you don't want to miss, head to the busy Plaza de la Cultura. Tour the ornate **National Theater** (p. 157) or get tickets for one of its many performing arts events. To see Costa Rica's collection of pre-Columbian gold artifacts, visit the adjacent **Gold Museum** (p. 157). If you have more time, a few blocks away are the **National Museum** (p. 157), **National Artisans Market** (p. 157), and **Jade Museum** (p. 157). And last but not least, sports fans can enjoy a walk around Parque Metropolitano La Sabana to see the impressive National Stadium, home to Costa Rica's mighty fútbol team.

Liberia/Guanacaste Province

One Week Itinerary: Omitted. Trip ends in Grecia/Atenas.

Two Week Itinerary: Liberia/Guanacaste Province – Days 12-14

If you're continuing on for more than a week, the last stop of your two-week trip takes you to another completely different area of the country, the Province of Guanacaste. About 4-5 hours northwest of the Central Valley, this region will seem like another world. Along the drive, you will notice the landscape change from steep hills of green rainforest to tropical dry forest with trees that even lose their leaves in times of drought. You will also see Costa Rica's plains, where long, straight highways run alongside vast sugarcane fields and cattle ranches.

Most visitors to Guanacaste come for its famed beaches and stay along the coast in places like Tamarindo, Playa Grande, Playa Flamingo, or Playa Hermosa (see Guanacaste Beaches, p. 102). As tourist destinations, these towns offer plenty of amenities and would make a good home base for exploring the region's cultural sights on day trips. But if you're coming to Costa Rica to really experience its authentic side, opt to stay in Guanacaste's capital city, Liberia.

While Liberia is best known for having one of the country's international airports, it is full of history and culture too. This bustling city doesn't draw a ton of tourists so the options for lodging are limited, but there are a few good choices. Check out one of the small hotels around the historic district (Calle Real), which are built in traditional nineteenth-century colonial style and are within walking distance to parks and historic churches.

A parade during one of the many festivals in Liberia

The Highlight

The authentic highlight of Guanacaste is a **horseback tour** (p. 160). Costa Rica's plainsmen, or *sabeneros*, are celebrated figures. Throughout the country, there are touring rodeos, prancing horse parades called *topes*, and even food brands that feature the outline of a brawny cowboy on their label. It is also not uncommon to see these iconic characters still hard at work herding cattle beside the road. To get in touch with your inner cowboy or cowgirl, there is no better way than on horseback. These tours are popular around the country, but especially common in Guanacaste. Whether you choose a tour near the beach or at a ranch in the *campo* (country), you are sure to experience a bit of authentic Costa Rica by riding along dirt roads and through small towns.

Other Activities and Attractions

A visit to the village of **Guaitil** (p. 160) near Santa Cruz will show you how pottery is made in the traditional pre-Columbian Chorotega style using outdoor ovens and natural dyes. During your time in Guanacaste, you'll see these colorful bowls, plates, and vases displayed proudly in local businesses as decorations. On your way back to Liberia or the beach, stop in the small city of Santa Cruz to eat at one of its many restaurants serving typical food or join the locals in the main square for an ice-cream cone.

For hiking and to see another one of Costa Rica's important historic sites, head to **Santa Rosa National Park** (p. 161). It was here that William Walker's filibusters were defeated in 1856, putting to rest Walker's plans to establish English-speaking colonies in Costa Rica. A historic ranch house within the park serves as a museum for the battle and showcases memorabilia from the time period. The park also hosts a vast tropical dry forest full of wildlife and some secluded beaches, making it a great place to spend the day.

While not a cultural sight, another great attraction that will have you exploring Guanacaste's small towns is **Rincon de la Vieja National Park** (p. 160). Rincon, located just a short drive from Liberia, is one of a set of volcanos in the Cordillera de Guanacaste mountain range. What makes the park unique are its steam vents, bubbling mud pots, and sulfur springs, which reach scalding temperatures due to this active volcano's geothermal energy. The park can be accessed via two ranger stations, Las Pailas on the western side and Santa María on the eastern side.

Other attractions in the area worth a visit are the **Llanos de Cortéz Waterfall** (p. 160), a large and elegant waterfall near the town of Bagaces, or **Las Pumas Rescue Center** (p. 160) in Cañas, where you can see monkeys, river otters, pumas, and other big cats.

3

ADVENTURE

Costa Rica's rugged landscape of steep mountains and wild jungle is a natural playground for the adrenaline seeker. Packed into this small, yet diverse, country are raging rivers, gushing waterfalls, spooky caves, deep canyons, and even active volcanos. All the destinations we've selected below offer a variety of exciting excursions from rafting some of the country's fiercest white water to rappelling down a rushing waterfall. Whether you want to explore Costa Rica's adventurous side by land, water, or even air, your heart will definitely be pumping on this adventure-focused itinerary.

One Week Itinerary: Jacó (3 days) to La Fortuna (4 days). Recommended Airport: SJO. View transportation options for this itinerary on p. 132.

Two Week Itinerary: Jacó (4 days) to Monteverde (3 days) to La Fortuna (4 days) to Turrialba (3 days). Recommended Airport: SJO. View transportation options for this itinerary on p. 133.

Jacó

One Week Itinerary: Jacó – Days 1-3

Two Week Itinerary: Jacó – Days 1-4

Your first stop for adventure is the popular beach town of Jacó. Located on the central Pacific coast less than two hours from San José, Jacó has a concentration of extreme activities, making it a top destination for the active vacationer.

Jacó is one of Costa Rica's most developed towns and, therefore, has a range of accommodations, restaurants, and tour operators. It is one of the only places in Costa Rica where you'll find a few high rises and condos in addition to the usual small hotels and lodges. Shops and bars line the streets near the beach, and the downtown has a party scene, which can get rowdy at night. **Tip:** If you're looking for a little more seclusion, consider staying in the outskirts of town or the neighboring beach communities of Playa Herradura or Playa Hermosa.

The Highlight

With so many activities to choose from, everyone's adventure highlight will be different. That's why the highlight in Jacó is an **all-in-one adventure tour** (p. 161). Several companies offer these packages, which typically include two, three, or even four different activities in a single day. Commonly paired are zip lining, ATV or off-road "buggy" rides, horseback riding, hiking, and canyoning (waterfall rappelling), but others can be combined as well. These tours are especially great for families or groups of people traveling together who might have different interests.

Other Activities and Attractions

One of Jacó's most unique activities is a **crocodile tour** (p. 161) on the Tárcoles River. With the help of an experienced (some would say crazy) guide, you'll get up close and personal with crocs, some as long as the boat you're in. Have the camera handy as you may even be able to get an epic selfie with one of these giants.

Another popular activity in Jacó among thrill seekers is

a **mountain-biking tour** (p. 161). Local trails climb the surrounding hills to reveal gorgeous ocean and jungle views, and there's even a bike park nearby with jumps and see-saws. For a real challenge, join some of the best cyclists in the world at the Ruta de Los Conquistadores (Route of the Conquistadors). This coast-to-coast, annual three-day race starts in Jacó and crosses the country to the Caribbean, traversing some of Costa Rica's most difficult terrain in between.

To cool off but still get in some excitement, take a snorkel or dive excursion to **Tortuga Island** (p. 161). Less than an hour off the coast, this pristine island has surrounding reefs where you can swim through massive schools of grunts or jack fish while seeing puffers, jumping rays, and even whitetip reef sharks. Divers up for deeper waters can explore three different shipwreck sites as well as underwater caves, which are known for easy shark sightings. Visibility is best in the dry season (December to April).

Other adventure activities in the Jacó area include bungee jumping, sky diving, and parasailing. For the water lovers, there is jet skiing and world-class surfing and sportfishing.

Monteverde

One Week Itinerary: Skip Monteverde. Go directly to La Fortuna.

Two Week Itinerary: Monteverde – Days 5-7

If you're on a two-week adventure, stop in Monteverde for a few days of high-altitude fun on your way from Jacó to La Fortuna (about 3-4 hours).

The town of Monteverde, originally settled by Quakers

in the early 1950s, was for decades little more than a tract
of forest and farmland in the remote mountains. Over the
years as the word spread about its intriguing cloud forests
and rugged outdoor activities, Monteverde and the
neighboring Santa Elena began to develop. Although the
area has grown, it hasn't lost its charm. The peaceful,
small-town feel remains even with a sizeable selection of
amenities. Accommodations consist mostly of eco-lodges,
which range from budget-friendly choices (clustered
around downtown Santa Elena) to deluxe lodges on the
edge of the rainforest.

   Tip: Be sure to get a four-wheel-drive vehicle with
higher clearance if you're renting a car as the roads getting
to and from Monteverde are rough dirt. Read our
Transportation Guide (p. 133) for more information.

The Highlight

Due to its high elevation and location along the
Continental Divide, the Monteverde area hosts some of
the country's best cloud forest. Seeing the cloud forest may
not sound like much of an adventure, but trust us, it can
be absolutely heart pounding when you're flying over the
tree tops on a **canopy zip-line tour** (p. 168).

   Zip lining can be done all around Costa Rica but what
makes it so special in Monteverde is that the sport started
here. Back in the 1970s, some crafty graduate students
developed zip lining as a way to study the highly diverse
rainforest canopy. Years later, it has spread worldwide, but
Monteverde still has some of the best runs around. When
choosing a company, keep in mind that tours vary in
number of cables and platforms, length, height, and top
speeds. Some may include a ride on a tram or a Tarzan
swing, while others may have a Superman line, which will
have you gliding face-first through the sky. **Tip:** When
speeding through the clouds, temps can be on the cool side
so be sure to take some warmer clothes and a raincoat.

Feeling the rush on a zip-line tour in Monteverde

Other Activities and Attractions

Those looking for other ways to explore the cloud forest and canopy can try either a hanging bridge walk or a gondola ride on a cable car. On the area's hanging bridges, you'll hike along easy trails while traversing a series of narrow bridges, each of various lengths, hung with cables and trellises. The two major companies in Monteverde are **Selvatura** (p. 167) and **Sky Adventures** (p. 167). Since these bridges cross over valleys and deep gorges, you'll have a tree-top view, which is perfect for bird-watching and wildlife spotting. On a cable-car ride at Sky Adventures, you'll be able to sit back and relax while being towed up through the canopy and into the clouds, then can take a quicker route back on a zip line.

Back on solid ground, strap on a helmet and some goggles for an **ATV tour** (p. 166). Throttling through forested trails, farm fields, and small streams, you will be kicking up dirt, mud, and rock on some of Monteverde's most rugged terrain. Tours typically snake into the mountains stopping along the way to give you great views

of the Pacific coastline and even Arenal Volcano, one of
your next destinations.

Other things to do for the adventure seeker include
canyoning (waterfall rappelling) or hiking through one of
the nearby reserves like the **Santa Elena Cloud Reserve**
(p. 167), **Children's Eternal Rainforest** (p. 166),
Monteverde Cloud Forest Reserve (p. 167), or **Curi
Cancha** (p. 166). Or for an evening thrill, take a guided
night hike to see some of the many eerie creatures that
inhabit the trails after dark like snakes, scorpions, and
spiders.

La Fortuna

One Week Itinerary: La Fortuna – Days 4-7

Two Week Itinerary: La Fortuna – Days 8-11

The next stop in your adventure itinerary takes you to La
Fortuna in the northern mountains (about 4 hours from
Jacó and 3-4 hours from Monteverde). La Fortuna may be
best known for the huge, conical-shaped volcano nearby,
but there is much more to do here than just hike around
old lava fields. Adventure seekers will feel right at home
with the long to-do list, which covers everything from
speeding across a lake while kitesurfing to squirming
through a tight pass in a dark cavern.

La Fortuna is a medium-sized town with plenty of
restaurants and shops in the concentrated downtown, which
spreads out toward the famous Arenal Volcano and nearby
lake. Hotels are abundant and range from all-inclusive
resorts with thermal hot springs and volcano views to jungle
lodges and rustic cabins. A car would be helpful to have,
especially if you're staying outside the downtown, as
activities and attractions are spread throughout the area.

The Highlight

The adventure highlight in La Fortuna can be found on Costa Rica's largest lake, Lake Arenal. Spanning 85 sq km (33 sq miles), this vast, man-made body of water sits quietly next to the active Arenal Volcano, but don't let its peaceful demeanor fool you. With wind speeds reaching 48 km (30 miles) per hour in some areas, Lake Arenal is a prime spot for adrenaline-pumping water sports. Often compared to the Columbia River Gorge in the Pacific Northwest and Lake Garda in Italy, here you'll find some of the best and most consistent windsurfing and kitesurfing on the planet. For optimum conditions, visit during the dry season of December through March, when gusts are most consistent. Companies who rent equipment and give lessons (like **Tico Wind**, p. 164) are located on the western side of the lake.

If skimming over the water at 30 plus knots and getting massive air off the chop isn't for you, try something a little more low-key. Kayaking, stand-up paddleboarding, wakeboarding, and fishing are all available in the lake's calmer coves and bays.

Other Activities and Attractions

Another favorite activity in La Fortuna among active travelers is waterfall rappelling, sometimes called **canyoning** (p. 162). With the help of a well-trained guide, you'll have the chance to rappel up to 61 meters (200 feet) down a water-filled canyon using ropes, carabineers, and descenders. The views you'll enjoy on the hike into the canyon are always a highlight among travelers.

For those interested in caving, there's the **Venado Caves** (p. 164). Donning a headlamp and rubber boots, you'll spelunk through the darkness to discover ancient rock formations, bats, and spiders living in the massive cavern. Prepare to get dirty as you'll have to crawl through tight spaces and may have to wade through deep water.

Some extreme hiking can be found at **Cerro Chato** (p. 162), the dormant sister of the neighboring Arenal Volcano. The steep, 4 hour (2 hours each way) climb to the summit rewards you with a chance to peer into the green crater lake below. Those up for an even bigger challenge can descend the slippery trail into the crater for a chance to say they swam in a volcanic lake.

Other popular adventure activities in La Fortuna are hanging bridges, hiking or mountain biking around Arenal Volcano, horseback riding, **La Fortuna Waterfall** (p. 163), soaking in the area's natural **hot springs** (p. 162), zip lining, and **white-water rafting** (p. 164) along the Balsa, Toro, or Sarapiquí rivers. **Tip:** If you're staying longer than a week, save the white-water rafting for later in your trip. The two-week itinerary below takes you to the town of Turrialba, home to Costa Rica's most mighty river, the Pacuare.

Turrialba

One Week Itinerary: Omitted. Trip ends in La Fortuna.

Two Week itinerary: Turrialba – Days 12-14

For the final leg of your two-week vacation, make the drive east around Costa Rica's Central Valley to the mountains of the Atlantic slope (about 4 hours). Here, you'll find the small city of Turrialba set deep in a valley with steep mountains all around. Turrialba originally sustained itself on textiles and the farming of dairy, coffee, sugar cane, macadamia nuts, and various fruits. Although these trades are still a big part of life, tourism has increased in recent years due to Turrialba's growing reputation for adventure travel.

To say that elevation varies widely in Turrialba is an understatement. The peak of the nearby Turrialba Volcano towers over the valley at 3,300 meters (11,000 feet), while just 20 km (12 miles) away, the city center reaches only 640 meters (2,100 feet). Needless to say, with this mountainous topography, it is no wonder that there are some extreme sports around.

Downtown Turrialba is the hub of the area. Though it may be small, the city is bustling and has plenty of typical restaurants, shops, and markets set along the grid-patterned streets. Basic lodging is conveniently located right in the downtown, but for the best views, head to the charming ranches and bed and breakfasts in the rural hills surrounding the city.

The Highlight

The adventure highlight in Turrialba is **white-water rafting** (p. 174). This sport has been popular in the Turrialba area for decades but recently gained notoriety after some well-known publications like National Geographic and Outdoor Magazine named the local Pacuare River one of the best places to raft in the world.

With balmy air temperatures, no wetsuit will be necessary as you paddle and splash your way past undeveloped jungle and through rocky canyons, getting some of the best views of your life. The most popular run on the Pacuare River drops over 300 meters (1,000 feet), starting in the hills east of Turrialba and rushing all the way to the town of Siquirres. Along this 29 km (18 mile) stretch, you will encounter adrenaline-pumping rapids, ranging from class III to class IV. Generally, river conditions remains consistent year-round, but when heavy rains create expert-only, class V rapids, there is a tamer river nearby. The Pejibaye River doesn't swell as much as the Pacuare, has a shorter run, and provides easier class II and III rapids.

Splashing down the Pacuare River.
Photo courtesy of Tico's River Adventures.

Other Activities and Attractions

For a real drop in elevation, keep your eyes to the sky. **Parapente Turrialba** (p. 173) offers paragliding excursions where, with a qualified guide, you will be lifted off the nearby mountains by the breeze in a colorful parachute. Floating high above the valley, you'll enjoy outstanding views of the nearby volcanos while your heart races from the rush of being in flight.

Back on the ground, it is possible to get a closer look at these two volcanos. The **Turrialba Volcano** (p. 174), although closed at the time of this writing because of activity, is normally accessed from rustic trails in the village of La Central. **Irazú Volcano** (p. 173), farther to the west, has easier access through a ranger station at Irazú Volcano National Park. Here, there is a short, 200 meter (650 foot) trail from a parking lot to the main crater's observation deck. **Tip:** Irazú's crater is often clouded over so be sure to evaluate the weather before paying to enter the park.

Other activities in the area include extreme paintball

at **Paintball Extremo Turrialba** (p. 173), mountain
biking or hiking the area's steep roads and trails,
canyoning, zip lining, or the nearby **Parque Paraíso de
Volcanes** (p. 173), an adventure park and ropes course.

4

SURFING

In 1994, Costa Rica suddenly became famous for its great waves thanks to the movie *Endless Summer II*. In that film, a couple of champion surfers from the United States, Pat O'Connell and Robert "Wingnut" Weaver, explored some of the amazing surfing breaks that at the time were extremely hard to access. If you're reading this section, you've probably seen the film many times. Luckily, access to Costa Rica's top surf destinations has greatly improved since those days, and surfing in Costa Rica has evolved into a major tourist attraction. This itinerary will have you paddling out to some of those awesome spots featured in the movie, while showing you more recently discovered places, which have become popular in the years since.

One Week Itinerary: Tamarindo or Playa Grande and Nearby Beaches (7 days). Recommended Airport: LIR. View transportation options for this itinerary on p. 135.

Two Week Itinerary: Tamarindo or Playa Grande (7 days) to Santa Teresa (4 days) to Playa Hermosa (Jacó) (3 days). Recommended Airport: LIR. View transportation options for this itinerary on p. 135.

Tamarindo/Playa Grande

One Week Itinerary: Tamarindo/Playa Grande – 7 days

Two Week Itinerary: Tamarindo/Playa Grande – 7 days

If you're planning to spend most of your time in the water, catching waves, the northwestern Pacific coast is the perfect place to start. This region is brimming with surfing opportunities, whether you're just starting out or looking for the next big thrill. To see all the area's amazing surf beaches, use the central locations of either Tamarindo or Playa Grande as a home base and visit the many beaches up and down the coast on day trips. Both towns are located about an hour from the international airport in Liberia.

Tip: There's a lot of stellar surfing in this area of the country, which is why we suggest staying for a full week. If you really want to get everything in, opt to rent a car. Some of the beaches recommended below like Playa Avellanas and Playa Negra are more remote and best accessed with your own wheels. Though the roads are mostly flat in this area and you could easily get around without an SUV, one is recommended for toting around your board. For more information, read the Transportation Guide (p. 135).

In Tamarindo, you'll find tons of surf shops, a lively nightlife, lots of amenities, and plenty of like-minded surfers. The town has a broad spectrum of accommodations, ranging from surf camps and hostels to luxury condos and everything in between. As for surf conditions, the main beach in town, Playa Tamarindo, features a beach break, which is perfect for beginners and intermediates. This beach is extremely popular and can sometimes get very busy. For the more skilled, some reef breaks on the southern end and a river-mouth break on the northern side are always less congested.

The quieter community of Playa Grande sits just across the river from Tamarindo. People not looking for a scene may prefer staying here in one of the many vacation rentals or small hotels set among the mangroves. The beach in Grande is long and a lot less crowded than Tamarindo. Since it faces slightly south, picking up the swell, the waves are generally larger as well. There are great lefts, rights, and sometimes barreling waves best for intermediate and advanced surfers. The nice thing about Playa Grande is that it is just a quick paddle or boat ride across the narrow river to the much livelier Tamarindo.

Shredding the waves in Tamarindo

The Highlight

The surfing highlight of the area is literally right out of the movies. Just like in *Endless Summer II*, you'll take a boat trip north to the beaches inside the remote Santa Rosa National Park. There, you will find Playa Naranjo and the iconic Witch's Rock jutting from the sea as well as Playa Potrero Grande, also known as Ollie's Point. Both are world-class surf spots.

Witch's Rock has a sandy-bottom beach break, which creates its best barrels at high tide, while Ollie's Point, another 20 minute boat ride up the coast, experiences its best point break during low tide. This unique combination of conditions allows you to surf with the tide all day long, using the boat to rest as needed. A trip here is not for beginners, but more advanced surfers will surely experience a full day of surfing bliss. Surf trips can be arranged through one of the surf schools in Tamarindo or Playa Grande.

Other Nearby Surf Beaches

Playa Langosta: Only a few kilometers south of Tamarindo is Playa Langosta. Not as busy as Playa Tamarindo, this beach also features a river mouth. To the north of the river outlet are reef breaks. Due to the extremely rocky bottom, these breaks are best surfed at mid-tide or higher. To the south of the river is a long stretch of sandy beach with only the occasional rock outcropping. This part of the beach can produce nice, sometimes hollow, breaks.

Playa Avellanas: About a half hour south of Tamarindo is Playa Avellanas. Called Little Hawaii by the locals, this undeveloped beach has a mixture of nice reef and beach breaks, which are easily discovered by walking up and down the sand. A popular place to park is at Lola's, one of the only restaurants around. North of Lola's, there is also a river mouth, which produces bigger waves best surfed at low tide.

Playa Negra: Just 10 minutes south of Playa Avellanas is Playa Negra, which was also featured in *Endless Summer II*. This beach is known for having a consistent reef break no matter the tide or swell. It is more for intermediate-to-advanced surfers because of the rocks, but a sandier area, just a short walk to the south, is good for beginners too.

Santa Teresa

One Week Itinerary: Omitted. Trip ends in Tamarindo/Playa Grande.

Two Week Itinerary: Santa Teresa – Days 8-11

If you're continuing your surfing adventure for another week, head from Tamarindo to the southern Nicoya Peninsula to explore some more awesome breaks.

Santa Teresa and its sister town, Mal País (Bad Country), sort of blend together into one laid back surfers' paradise. It is a long, 4-5 hour drive with some rough road conditions along the way, but the surfing and vibe here are well worth the trip. These towns are not nearly as built up as Tamarindo, but still have plenty of surf shops, amenities, and a good nightlife. Accommodations range from hotels, surf camps, and hostels to vacation rentals, yoga retreats, and small resorts. **Tip:** If you get a rental car for Santa Teresa, make sure it has four-wheel drive for the bumpy ride to Mal País. Read more in the Transportation Guide (p. 136).

Because they're at the tip of the peninsula, the beaches around Santa Teresa tend to get the right combination of swell, wind, and currents, which make for some spectacular surfing. From south to north, you'll find Playa Carmen, which will satisfy everyone from beginners to pros, Playa Santa Teresa, which has more advanced breaks, and Playa Hermosa, which has the easiest conditions.

The Highlight

Playa Santa Teresa is the surfing highlight of the area. This beach is less crowded than Carmen and has barreling rights and lefts over some rocky areas when the swells are large. There are two really special breaks on the very northern end of Playa Santa Teresa, La Lora and Suck Rock. La Lora is a long stretch of white sand with a consistent beach break and very few rocks. For this reason, La Lora is often used for surf competitions. Suck Rock, just to the north of La Lora, is a fast right-hand point break, which can get double overhead before closing out with the right swell. Both are highly recommended for advanced surfers.

Other Nearby Surfing Beaches

Playa Carmen: Playa Carmen is a busy beach, which can sometimes have crowded waters. This is because Carmen attracts both beginners learning in the white water and more advanced surfers out challenging the swells. This beach break is best surfed at lower tides. Be sure to keep north of the parking lot as it gets rocky to the south.

Playa Hermosa: One of the many beaches in Costa Rica with this same name, Playa Hermosa near Santa Teresa offers easier beach breaks and milder riptides so is great for beginners. That said, there are some nice point breaks formed by rocks that jut out into the surf, best left to the more advanced. Playa Hermosa tends to be less busy because it is slightly out of town to the north.

Playa Montezuma and Playa Cabuya: When the waves are closing out on the beaches near Santa Teresa, surfers can head east to Playa Montezuma or Playa Cabuya. Located on the sheltered side of the peninsula, these beaches will have more manageable waves during a good southern swell.

Playa Hermosa (Jacó)

One Week Itinerary: Omitted. Trip ends in Tamarindo/Playa Grande.

Two Week Itinerary: Playa Hermosa (Jacó) – Days 12-14

From the nearby town of Montezuma, take a speedboat taxi from the Nicoya Peninsula to the mainland, arriving in Playa Herradura. The ride will take only about an hour, cutting off a half day of travel over land. From here, go just south to Playa Hermosa, where you'll spend the last few days of your two-week trip. **Tip:** Those with a rental car either can drive around the peninsula or take a car ferry from Paquera to Puntarenas. Read more in the Transportation Guide (p. 136).

Playa Hermosa means Beautiful Beach in Spanish and after spending some time at this majestic 7 km (4 mile) stretch of sand, you'll understand how it got its name. With a smooth-bottom beach break and some of the most consistent and powerful waves in the country, Playa Hermosa is one of Costa Rica's most iconic surfing beaches. The beach itself is known for having riptides and more advanced waves, but beginners can still find opportunity on the inside waves that develop, if they are careful.

Another draw of Playa Hermosa is that it offers a relaxed atmosphere and smaller community, but is just 8 km (5 miles) from the bustling town of Jacó. In Jacó, you'll find plenty to do through the many tour operators, bars, restaurants, and shops. Playa Hermosa, although smaller, has a good selection of beachside hotels, inns, vacation rentals, and small resorts. There are also some lodges and bed and breakfasts set into the nearby hills, which offer more privacy.

Playa Hermosa, beautiful beach, beautiful surf

The Highlight

The highlight of your time at Playa Hermosa is the personal connection you can have with the sea. This may sound corny but the long, uncrowded beach offers a unique opportunity to find your own spot and feel like you're the only one out there. Maybe it is while the sun rises or sets or during the heat of the day, but the complete isolation and solitude you can experience while floating on your board at Playa Hermosa is truly special. It is these moments that will give you time to reflect back on the surfing adventures you had in Costa Rica and get you thinking about planning more.

Other Nearby Surfing Beaches and Breaks

Playa Jacó: Playa Jacó is a good option for beginners and has easier breaks thanks to the shelter of the bay. Some of the better breaks along the beach can get very crowded, especially on weekends with the influx of locals from San José.

Roca Loca: Located below the large cliff, just south of Jacó Beach, Roca Loca (Crazy Rock) may be a better spot to watch and get inspired than to actually surf. Local experts hit up this nice right when the waves are overhead, dodging the massive rock in front of them while they drop in.

Playa Esterillos Oeste: About 15 km (9 miles) south of Playa Hermosa is the quiet town of Esterillos Oeste. Surfing here can be fun and relaxing since it tends to be deserted. This beach has a nice beach break off the rock shelf, which forms slowly and doesn't get too steep.

More Costa Rica Surf Spots: If you suddenly forget that you have a plane to catch, like a lot of vacationing surfers do, send an e-mail to the office and continue your surfing journey. Farther down the Pacific coast, you'll find excellent waves in Dominical, Zancudo, and Pavones. And if you want to take your surfing adventure coast to coast, the Caribbean side offers even more opportunities in Puerto Limón, Cahuita, and Puerto Viejo de Talamanca.

5

WILDLIFE

Wildlife enthusiasts could spend months or even years traveling around Costa Rica, constantly discovering new species. Among the country's some 250 types of mammals, 900 types of birds, 220 types of reptiles, and 190 types of amphibians are monkeys, sloths, poison dart frogs, pumas, toucans, and crocodiles, just to name a few. Because most travelers are on a time constraint, we have selected some of the most biologically rich areas of the country where sightings are relatively easy through self-exploration or guided tours. We have also included destinations with wildlife rescue and rehabilitation centers. Visiting these organizations will give you the chance to see rare rainforest animals that can be difficult to find in the wild like jaguars, pit vipers, collared anteaters, and Scarlet Macaw parrots.

*Only Included in
Two Week Itinerary

One Week Itinerary: Tortuguero (3 days) to Manuel Antonio (4 days). Recommended Airport: SJO. View transportation options for this itinerary on p. 137.

Two Week Itinerary: *This itinerary starts in Puerto Viejo de Talamanca instead of Tortuguero.* Puerto Viejo de Talamanca (3 days) to Tortuguero (3 days) to Manuel Antonio (4 days) to Drake Bay (4 days). Recommended Airport: SJO. View transportation options for this itinerary on p. 138.

Puerto Viejo de Talamanca

One Week Itinerary: Skip Puerto Viejo de Talamanca. Go directly to Tortuguero.

Two Week Itinerary: Puerto Viejo de Talamanca – Days 1-3

For those on a two-week wildlife excursion, you'll start your adventure on the southern Caribbean coast in Puerto Viejo de Talamanca (4 hours from San José). While boasting many tourist amenities, this area is enveloped in steamy lowland rainforest, making it the perfect place to spot wildlife. In addition to the monkeys, sloths, and birds you will likely spot along hiking trails, beach paths, or even from the road, Puerto Viejo also has some of the best wildlife centers in the country.

The laid-back beach town of Puerto Viejo has a small but busy downtown right next to the palm-tree-lined Playa Negra (Black Beach). Along the narrow streets, you will find hotels and hostels, many small businesses, grocery stores, and a good concentration of restaurants and bars. In fact, the area hosts around 90 different eateries, which like accommodations, spread southward into the beach communities of Playa Cocles, Playa Chiquita, and Playa Punta Uva. Wildlife seekers may enjoy staying in one of these quieter communities to be surrounded by rainforest. Beachfront bungalows, B&Bs, boutique hotels, and many vacation rentals dot the road leading south to the quiet village of Manzanillo.

A Word of Caution: Always be aware of your surroundings in Puerto Viejo and never leave your belongings unattended. Puerto Viejo is generally safe but theft and crime are an occasional problem. It is best to be extra cautious by leaving your valuables locked in the safe of your hotel room. When going to the beach, take only your towel and sunscreen or make sure someone is watching your bag when you're swimming. Finally, a good practice no matter where you are in Costa Rica is to always lock your rental car and never leave anything in sight.

The Highlight

The wildlife highlight in Puerto Viejo is the **Jaguar Rescue Center** (p. 171) in Playa Chiquita. Although named after its first resident, a jaguar, this rescue and rehabilitation center has much more than jungle cats. On a guided tour, you will see sloths, monkeys, deer, anteaters, snakes, frogs, insects, and lots of different bird species, including parrots, toucans, and owls. Unique cages that are left open during the day provide close-up views, but even more exciting is the chance to enter one of the large enclosures to hang out with the monkeys. The guided tours are extremely informative, which is no surprise since the center was started by a biologist.

A baby anteater on a volunteer at Jaguar Rescue Center

Other Activities and Attractions

Popular wildlife hikes near Puerto Viejo include the **Gandoca-Manzanillo National Wildlife Refuge** (p. 171) about 15 minutes to the south and **Cahuita National Park** (p. 156) about 20 minutes to the north. Both provide ample opportunities to see howler monkeys, sloths, and snakes like the bright yellow eyelash pit viper. Trails in both parks are relatively flat and easy, though it is recommended that you explore the more remote Gandoca-Manzanillo Refuge with a guide.

For the ultimate sloth experience, head to the **Sloth Sanctuary** (p. 156) in Cahuita. This well-known rescue and rehabilitation center specifically focuses on helping Costa Rica's two sloth species, all while educating the public about them. Part of the tour is a guided canoe ride along a nearby river where you'll likely see howler monkeys, lizards, birds, butterflies, and of course sloths. Another part will have you visiting the resident sloths, including a stop in the nursery where you can see babies getting nursed back to health.

For the bird lover, the **Ara Project's** (p. 170) release site in Manzanillo will fulfill your wildest dreams. Here, you will see how Costa Rica's most threatened parrots, endangered Great Green Macaws, are successfully being reintroduced into the wild. Finally, for those looking to explore marine life, prime snorkeling and diving sites are located off the nearby coral reefs in both Cahuita and Manzanillo.

Tortuguero

One Week Itinerary: Tortuguero – Days 1-3

Two Week Itinerary: Tortuguero – Days 4-6

One-week vacationers will go straight from San José to Tortuguero to begin their wildlife search, while two-week vacationers will head up the coast from Puerto Viejo to Tortuguero for their second stop.

Located on Costa Rica's northern Caribbean coast (a 4-5 hour drive from San José or 1 hr. flight, and a 4-5 hour drive from Puerto Viejo), the remote village of Tortuguero is accessible only by small plane or boat taxi. See the Transportation Guide (p. 137) for more information about getting to Tortuguero.

Within the varied landscape of canal, mangrove, rainforest, and beach, you'll find a myriad of animals. Wading birds, crocodiles, manatees, monkeys, river otters, parrots, anteaters, sloths, and even big cats can be found in the swampy habitat, but the wildlife that Tortuguero is most famous for is turtles. Four types of sea turtles nest along the area's beaches, and the Sea Turtle Conservancy has even named this tiny village the most important nesting site for endangered green sea turtles in the Western Hemisphere.

Though you'll feel a world away in the wild jungle surrounds, the popular destination of Tortuguero is well traveled and has plenty of the comforts of home. Accommodations consist mostly of eco-lodges and cabins, but there are also a few small resorts and more upscale lodges. **Tip:** Because this area is difficult to get to and also to get around once you arrive, vacation packages often include transportation to and from San José, lodging, meals, and tours.

The Highlight

The wildlife highlight of Tortuguero is a miracle that happens under the cover of darkness: the nesting of endangered sea turtles. With the help of a licensed guide, you can witness this mysterious act along the beaches of **Tortuguero National Park** (p. 172). Using the light of the moon and red flashlights, you'll be able to get surprisingly close to these clumsy creatures while they dig holes and lay their eggs in the very same sand from which they hatched.

The two best seasons for turtle viewing are July through October (for Atlantic green sea turtles) and March through May (for gigantic leatherback sea turtles). If your travel plans don't coincide with a nesting event, don't fret. It is still possible to see an occasional nester or some recent hatchlings making their way to the sea during the early morning hours. For those wanting to learn even more about the lifecycle of the different turtle species that visit the area, there is a small **Sea Turtle Conservancy Center** (p. 172) in town.

Other Activities and Attractions

Boat tours as well as canoe and kayak rentals are great ways to explore the wildlife of Tortuguero's network of brackish waterways. Within Tortuguero National Park are four waterway trails, which can be accessed by motor-less watercraft. **Tip:** If you choose to paddle through the park's canals on your own, be sure to stop at the ranger station to get a map.

For those who would rather stay on solid ground, the park also has a limited land-trail system, which consists of the 2 km (1.25 mile) Gavilán loop. Optional guides for the short hike are available through the ranger station and will help ensure you see hidden wildlife, which you would normally pass by, like roosting bats or colonies of arboreal termites.

Another short but more difficult hike can be found at Turtle Hill. Leading to the highest point in the area at 120 meters (almost 400 feet), a trek to the top of this small mountain will give you an excellent view of Tortuguero village below. The trail is accessible via a 10-15 minute boat ride from town. This hill is a great place to see some of the more than 400 different bird species spotted in the area like the colorful Keel-billed Toucan or the rare Purple-throated Fruitcrow.

Tip: Always keep your eyes open and camera ready, as in Tortuguero, you are constantly surrounded by nature. Although you will no doubt have many great sightings during tours and organized outings, you may be surprised with what you can discover right at your hotel, during dinner, and on the boat ride to and from the mainland.

Manuel Antonio

One Week Itinerary: Manuel Antonio – Days 4-7

Two Week Itinerary: Manuel Antonio – Days 7-10

After exploring the marshy canals of Tortuguero, head across the country to Manuel Antonio on the central Pacific coast. Here, you will find some of Costa Rica's most beautiful beaches and rainforest teeming with wildlife. From Tortuguero, Manuel Antonio is best accessed by small plane to the neighboring town of Quepos, though you can also travel by land if you don't mind a longer trip. See the Transportation Guide (p. 137) for more information.

Manuel Antonio is a tourist-based town built along the hilly seashore with a wide range of amenities and attractions. Although it hosts everything from five-star resorts to inexpensive hostels, white-linen restaurants to hot-dog stands, it still manages to fit into the surrounding jungle. Everything seems to be tucked into the rainforest, and wildlife like sloths, tropical birds, and especially monkeys can be spotted throughout town, even from your hotel balcony.

The Highlight

Manuel Antonio's wildlife highlight is **Manuel Antonio National Park** (p. 165). This is Costa Rica's busiest park, and although it sometimes has a long line of visitors waiting to enter, wildlife is still easy to spot. Most notably, the park is home to three of the four types of monkeys that can be found in Costa Rica. White-faced monkeys are the most commonly seen species. These boisterous primates can be found throughout the park, even near the busy beaches interacting with people. The other two types, howler monkeys and endangered gray-crowned squirrel monkeys, tend to be shyer and are most easily spotted by sound, howlers by their loud groans and squirrels by their high-pitched chirps.

A gray-crowned squirrel monkey in Manuel Antonio

While Manuel Antonio National Park is best known for its monkeys, other animals also can be found among the 1,983 hectares (4,900 acres) of landmass and 55,000 hectares (135,908 acres) of marine reserve. Species include three-toed sloths, raccoons, spiny-tailed iguanas, hermit crabs, and hundreds of birds like the Blue-crowned Motmot or Lineated Woodpecker. *Closed Mondays during the low season (July 1 – Nov. 30).*

Tip: Since the park can get extremely crowded, wildlife viewing is best in the early mornings or on the less frequented trails off the main "avenue." When hiking the trails, walk slowly, scan the area, and listen for subtle movements to see the most. Animals typically freeze when they hear you approach, and unsuspecting tourists often walk noisily past while troops of monkeys hide silently in the trees right above them.

Other Activities and Attractions

The **Isla Damas Estuary** (p. 164), just north of Manuel Antonio, is another area that provides easy wildlife viewing. On a guided sea kayak or motorboat tour through these tidal mangroves, you will likely see white-faced monkeys, Halloween crabs, sloths, green iguanas, and spectacled caimans. Lucky visitors might also spot snakes like the boa constrictor or rare mammals like the silky or collared anteater.

For hiking, head south to **Hacienda Barú** (p. 158), a former cattle ranch turned lodge and nature reserve about 45 minutes from Manuel Antonio. This private reserve has four, mostly flat trails, which traverse primary and secondary rainforest, fields, and streams. In addition to monkeys and birds, at Hacienda Barú, it is possible to see paca (a large rabbit-like animal), white-nosed coati (a raccoon-like animal usually found in large groups along the forest floor), and maybe even Scarlet Macaws. These endangered parrots only recently returned to the area after nearly becoming extinct due to hunting and habitat loss.

Other wildlife-related activities near Manuel Antonio include a visit to the **Kids Saving the Rainforest wildlife sanctuary** (p. 164), hiking in **Rainmaker Park** (p. 165), a catamaran and snorkel tour, or **whale and dolphin watching** (p. 159) off the coast of Marino Ballena National Park in Uvita.

Drake Bay

One Week Itinerary: Omitted. Trip ends in Manuel Antonio.

Two Week Itinerary: Drake Bay – Days 11-14

The last stop on your two-week wildlife extravaganza will take you to Costa Rica's most biologically rich destination, the Osa Peninsula. Drake Bay, which sits at the northwestern corner of this large tract of protected rainforest, is an excellent jumping-off point for exploring the wildest part of the country and all its inhabitants. If this area looks familiar, don't be surprised; you've probably seen these same forests and oceans on TV channels like Discovery, National Geographic, and Animal Planet.

In the village of Drake Bay, you will find rustic cabins alongside modern lodges and small resorts as well as a few scattered restaurants and mini-groceries. These establishments, set in the jungle, are spread out around the beautiful cove where local fishing boats bob with the swells. Because the town is so remote, many of the accommodations have their own restaurants and include all meals with their packages.

The best way to access this area from Manuel Antonio is to take a shuttle south to the town of Sierpe (2 hours) and then a short riverboat ride. Once you snake through the murky waters of the Río Sierpe, your boat will venture into the mighty Pacific Ocean and follow the coast south before finally landing in the bay. After your stay, a small airstrip in Drake provides daily flights back San José, saving you an otherwise long travel day by land. For more information, read the Transportation Guide (p. 140).

The Highlight

When the sun sets in Drake Bay, the rainforest plays a symphony of sounds. At dusk, it may start with a few chirping frogs then suddenly transform into a concert of noisy creatures. For the wildlife highlight in Drake Bay, stay up late to see firsthand how the jungle comes alive after dark. On a **night walk tour** (p. 160), you will trek through the jungle with only the light of a headlamp. Along the way, a knowledgeable guide will point out forest dwellers you didn't even know existed. Insects that resemble rotting leaves or caterpillars that mimic poisonous snakes. Bats that make their own tents using palm fronds and even fungi that glows in the dark. Among these magical creatures, you'll likely see some much more familiar species too, like snakes, spiders, frogs, beetles, and even nocturnal mammals like armadillos, opossums, and kinkajous.

Tip: Only a few operators offer these tours. Book in advance through your lodge and schedule yours for one of the first nights you're in town. The appreciation and knowledge you'll gain from the experience will have you noticing much more during the rest of your stay.

Other Activities and Attractions

Drake Bay provides easy access to Central America's largest tract of lowland rainforest, **Corcovado National Park** (p. 159). Guided day trips arrive inside the park by boat to both the San Pedrillo and Sirena Ranger Stations and provide excellent opportunities to see some of Costa Rica's rarest birds and animals. Some standouts that you may see on the trails include Costa Rica's largest land mammal, the endangered Baird's tapir, the boar-like white-lipped peccary, and even the black-crowned squirrel monkey, a different subspecies from those found in Manuel Antonio. For more adventurous travelers, overnight stays in one of these rustic ranger stations are available if booked in advance.

Another popular boat tour will take you to **Caño Island** (p. 159) about 16 km (10 miles) offshore. Not only is Caño Island a great place to snorkel or dive, but the diversity in the warm ocean waters around the island will likely have you pointing out dolphins, flying fish, sea turtles, rays, and even humpback whales.

Other activities for good wildlife sightings include kayaking, mangrove tours, a river float trip, or a hike along the coast to the remote San Josecito beach for snorkeling right offshore.

6

BIRDING

Almost 900 types of birds have been identified in Costa Rica, an astonishing amount for such a small country. What draws so many different species are Costa Rica's varied climate, geography, and rich biodiversity. Though one would expect to need a lot of time to see everything, the country's best birding locations can easily be explored in just one or two weeks. In fact, in a single day, birders can enjoy a morning session in tropical lowlands and an afternoon in high-elevation cloud forest. In this itinerary, we will take you to some of Costa Rica's birding hotspots where you can check dozens, if not hundreds, of different species off your life list, all while getting a taste of the country's most diverse landscapes.

One Week Itinerary: Puerto Viejo de Sarapiquí (4 days) to San Gerardo de Dota (3 days). Recommended Airport: SJO. View transportation options for this itinerary on p. 141.

Two Week Itinerary: Puerto Viejo de Sarapiquí (4 days) to San Gerardo de Dota (3 days) to Costa Ballena (5 days) to Tárcoles (2 days). Recommended Airport: SJO. View transportation options for this itinerary on p. 141.

Puerto Viejo de Sarapiquí (Caribbean Slope)

One Week Itinerary: Puerto Viejo de Sarapiquí – Days 1-4

Two Week Itinerary: Puerto Viejo de Sarapiquí – Days 1-4

Begin your Costa Rica birding adventure in the steamy Caribbean lowlands of Puerto Viejo de Sarapiquí, located about 1.5 hours north of San José. Surrounded by agricultural fields of banana, pineapple, and cattle, here you'll find dense protected jungle made up of several reserves. Within this massive island of tropical forest lives an abundance of bird species, with nearly 500 identified thus far. With those numbers, it won't be hard to rack up an impressive list of your own.

The largest town in the area is Puerto Viejo de Sarapiquí, which has a slightly built up downtown near the banks of the Sarapiquí River. The town itself is primarily commerce based, supplying the local farms and businesses but also can be a great place to explore the local culture. There are many small restaurants and shops dispersed throughout the center of town and a few hotels as well. But most vacationers, especially birders, choose to stay in one of the handful of eco-lodges that border the bird-rich jungle.

Tip: For this itinerary, a four-wheel-drive rental car is recommended. This will give you the most flexibility for bird-watching because many of the birding sites are spread out and located in very rural areas. Being able to explore these spots on your own time without having to rely on a tour van or taxi will make the experience much more enjoyable.

Birding Highlight

La Selva Biological Station (p. 169) is the birding highlight of the area. Situated just outside town at the fork between the Sarapiquí and Puerto Viejo Rivers, this 1,614 hectare (3,988 acre) reserve has become famous worldwide for its amazing biodiversity. Among the old growth and tropical wet forests, you'll find scientists studying everything from frogs and ferns to bats and birds to nutrient cycling and carbon sequestration. Although research is king here, there is also room for the everyday birder. Overnight guests can explore the reserve's entire 56 km (35 mile) trail system, while day visitors can take a guided tour to see a few of the more easily accessible loops.

Some of the hundreds of birds you may encounter at La Selva include the Collared Aracari, Keel-billed Toucan, Snowy Cotinga, Crimson-fronted Parakeet, Purple-throated Fruitcrow, Passerini's Tanager, Fasciated Antshrike, and if you are extremely lucky, the Bare-necked Umbrellabird.

Other Birding Activities

Another nearby reserve worth a visit is the **Tirimbina Biological Reserve** (p. 170). This 345 hectare (852 acre) plot in the town of La Virgen contains similar habitat to La Selva but has an impressive hanging bridge over the river, which puts you at eye level with species like the Broad-billed Motmot, White-crowned Parrot, Red-capped Manakin, Tawny-faced Gnatwren, and Red-throated Ant-tanager.

For another great way to bird, head to the main dock in Sarapiquí for a riverboat tour to see the Mangrove Swallow, Gray-rumped Swift, Montezuma Oropendola, Amazon Kingfisher, Green Heron, Anhinga, and maybe even a pair of endangered Great Green Macaws flying overhead.

Sarapiquí has lots of reserves that are great for birding but don't overlook what you can find near farm fields and side roads. The Variable Seedeater, Red-winged Blackbird, Broad-winged Hawk, Blue-black Grassquit, Paint-billed Crake, and many others can be spotted along these forest edges. Finally, if you're into photography, you don't want to miss the **Nature Pavilion** (p. 170) in La Virgen. The Nature Pavilion has transformed biologically stale palm fields into vibrant rainforest that attracts birds with strategically placed trees, feeders, and perches. The covered deck is also great for those rainy days, which may otherwise be a washout.

San Gerardo de Dota
(High-elevation Mountains)

One Week Itinerary: San Gerardo de Dota – Days 5-7

Two Week Itinerary: San Gerardo de Dota – Days 5-7

The next stop on this feather-filled journey is the unique cloud forest habitat of San Gerardo de Dota to see high-altitude specialists like the Collared Redstart, Sooty Thrush, Hairy Woodpecker, Torrent Tyrannulet, Fiery-throated Hummingbird, and most notably the amazing Resplendent Quetzal. From Puerto Viejo de Sarapiquí, the scenic drive back through the mountains will be 3-4 hours.

San Gerardo de Dota is a quiet village that sits deep in a valley bordering the swift-moving Savegre River. In San Gerardo, you'll find a handful of eco-lodges, all which offer great birding opportunities on landscaped grounds. Additionally, the town's dirt roads and riverside trails offer some nicely varied habitat, including hardwood forest, riparian edges, grassy pasture, and flowering gardens. Because of the altitude (around 2,195 meters or 7,200 feet), the weather is quite cool compared to the Caribbean lowlands of Sarapiquí, sometimes dipping into the 60s°F (16°C) at night. Be sure to pack some warmer clothes.

Birding Highlight

The birding highlight of San Gerardo de Dota is the Resplendent Quetzal. This iconic trogon species with iridescent green and red coloring and magnificent tail feathers, which can reach up to 30 inches (76 cm) long, is especially recognizable. Unlike other cloud forests in Costa Rica, like Monteverde, Resplendent Quetzals can readily be found in San Gerardo year-round and you are almost guaranteed a sighting, especially when hiring a guide. The Quetzals feed mostly on small fruits like wild avocado, and local guides know the exact locations around town where they are commonly spotted. If you travel in late March or April, you'll have the most luck, as this is breeding season and the Quetzals are most active.

A male Resplendent Quetzal
Photo courtesy of Jeffrey Muñoz, Distinctive Expeditions.

Other Birding Activities

Other activities in San Gerardo de Dota that will interest the birder include hiking in the nearby **Los Quetzales National Park** (p. 172). This massive 5,000 hectare (12,000 acre) swath of land has even higher elevation trails, which dip into the valley. A shorter loop, the Sendero Ojo de Agua to Camino Público, can be explored in a half day.

This trail starts above the timberline, showing birds like the Volcano Junco and Timberline Wren, and descends steeply into thick forest where Ruddy Treerunners and Yellow-winged Vireos are more likely found. The hike down is very steep so a return to the ranger station via the dirt road (Camino Público) is recommended. Birders with more time can make the longer 9 km (5.6 mile) trek from the ranger station back to San Gerardo de Dota to see similar habitat.

For a less difficult hike right in town, follow the path leading past the trout farm to the Savegre River Waterfall (about 1.5 hours each way). Although the hike is along relatively flat terrain, there are some rickety footbridges to cross so use caution.

Enthusiastic birders could also spend hours at local feeders and gardens, counting the different hummingbird species, like the Volcano Hummingbird, Magenta-throated Woodstar, or Scintillant Hummingbird, or take a night walk to identify the calls of the Costa Rican Pigmy-Owl or Dusky Nightjar.

Costa Ballena (South Pacific Slope)

One Week Itinerary: Omitted. Trip ends in San Gerardo de Dota.

Two Week Itinerary: Costa Ballena – Days 8-12

If you're continuing your birding vacation for another week, head from the mountains of San Gerardo de Dota to the heels of the Pacific slope, about 2 hours away. In the area known as the Costa Ballena (Whale Coast), you'll find steep mountains slanting down to touch the sea. This varied elevation not only attracts a lot of birds unique to southwestern Costa Rica but also makes it possible to explore the rich diversity of shore and sea birds as well.

The Costa Ballena is made up of the beach towns of Dominical, Uvita, and Ojochal. These small towns are more spread out, but between the three of them, offer accommodations and restaurants to satisfy a wide range of comforts and budgets. For the best sightings, birders should take advantage of one of the lodges or hotels located in the less populated, jungle-rich hills.

Birding Highlight

Because the Costa Ballena takes you to the shores of the mighty Pacific Ocean, the birding highlight here is the opportunity to check a number of seabirds off your list. A visit to **Marino Ballena National Park** (Whale National Marine Park) (p. 158) in Uvita will turn up species like the Magnificent Frigatebird, Brown Booby, Brown Pelican, and maybe even migrating Spotted Sandpipers, Black-bellied Plovers, and Surfbirds. On land, it is easy to scout from the long and rocky, whale-tail-shaped sandbar or you could take a kayak to the craggy islets just off the coast.

For seaworthy birders, a boat trip to Caño Island farther south off the Osa Peninsula can turn up even more. The island itself doesn't host a large population of birds, but with a little luck, on the way to and from you'll spot some pelagics like the Blue-footed Booby, Red-footed Booby, Brown Noddy, and even some Storm Petrels. Depending on the season, you can also encounter several tern and gull species like the Royal Turn, Bridled Turn, or Laughing Gull. And as an added bonus, it is not uncommon for these boat tours to pass pods of spotted and spinner dolphins along with the occasional migrating humpback whale. Boat tours can be booked in Uvita.

Other Birding Activities

Back on land, there is a lot to explore within the Costa Ballena. In Dominical, **Hacienda Barú Wildlife Refuge**

(p. 158) provides 7 km (4.3 miles) of trails through primary
and secondary forest, mangrove, grassland, and even
beach. Here, you will see birds like the Cherrie's Tanager,
Spot-crowned Euphonia, Great Curassow, Black-
mandibled Toucan, and Common Potoo, as well as many
raptor species like the Roadside Hawk, Crested Caracara,
King Vulture, and Laughing Falcon.

To the south in Uvita, you will find two more common
birding stops at **Oro Verde Nature Reserve** (p. 158) and
Rancho La Merced (p. 159). These private reserves can
turn up sightings of the Fiery-billed Aracari, Golden-naped
Woodpecker, Baird's or Violaceous Trogon, Turquoise
Cotinga, Charming Hummingbird, and Red-lored Parrot.

After exploring the trails around Uvita and Dominical,
determined birders can drive an hour or two south in
search of some rare species around the Osa Peninsula and
Golfo Dulce like the Brown-throated Parakeet, Slate-
colored Seedeater, and Rusty-margined Flycatcher.
Piedras Blancas National Park (p. 158) near the town of
La Gamba is a great jumping-off point for exploring this
area. Although this vast parcel of rainforest touches a few
different towns and does not have an official park
entrance, access is available through trails maintained by
the Esquinas Rainforest Lodge. **Tip:** Keep an eye out for
the Wattled Jaçana, usually found in Panama, which is
commonly spotted around the rice fields near La Gamba.

Tárcoles (Pacific Slope)

One Week Itinerary: Omitted. Trip ends in San Gerardo
de Dota.

Two Week Itinerary: Tárcoles – Days 13-14

For the two-week birder, the last stop on your tour
through Costa Rica takes you about 2 hours north of the

Costa Ballena to Tárcoles. Located just 70 km (44 miles) southwest of the San José international airport, Tárcoles sits in a transition zone between the tropical dry forests of northwestern Costa Rica and the tropical wet forests that you will have visited to the south. This unique habitat draws species from both regions and is known as one of the best birding sites in the entire country. The area is also known for easy Scarlet Macaw sightings, and flashes of red, blue, and yellow feathers overhead are a likely treat.

A Scarlet Macaw feeding in an almond tree

Tárcoles is a small ocean-side fishing village at the mouth of a river with a lot of local culture and character. Apart from a few eco-lodges (which focus on birding) and family-run restaurants, Tárcoles offers travelers few amenities. Those looking for more to choose from, or who have saturated their travel companions with too many birding excursions, may want to explore the tourist destinations of Playa Herradura and Jacó, just to the south. These towns offer a plethora of activities, accommodations, and beautiful beaches (see Surfing, p. 47, and Adventure, p. 29).

Birding Highlight

Carara National Park (p. 161) stands out as the birding highlight of the Tárcoles region. This park, which encompasses 5,242 hectares (12,953 acres), not only sits at the crossroads of the wet and dry forests, but different parts of the trail system contain elements of each. The most popular trail is the Universal Loop, which has paved paths and resting benches, making it easily accessible for birders with disabilities. The trail takes you through some nicely shaded forest with a mixture of tall trees and shrubby undergrowth, and also has two offshoots, the Quebrada Bonita and Areceas. These trails are easy to moderate in difficulty and pass through even thicker secondary and old-growth rainforest. Along all these paths, it is possible to spot the Blue-crowned and Long-tailed Manakin, Great Tinamou, and Streak-chested Antpitta, as well as up to five different trogon species.

Another trail, the Meandrica, is located off the highway and starts about 2 km (1.2 miles) north of the main ranger station. Also called the River Trail, this path meanders alongside a river through varied habitat of forest, open pasture, and even a crocodile-filled lagoon. The trail is a great place to look for the Magpie Jay, Scarlet Macaw, Orange-collared Manakin, Turquoise-browed Motmot, Yellow-billed Cotinga, Great Kiskadee, Boat-billed Heron, and Black-bellied or Riverside Wren. Be sure to inquire with park rangers for best access and secure parking when visiting the Meandrica Trail, as it is isolated from the rest of the park's facilities.

Other Birding Activities

Other than Carara National Park, there are several key

places to bird. For early mornings before park headquarters open, walk the road leading to the Bijagual Waterfall, just south of the park entrance. This road hosts many of the same species you would find inside the park and generally doesn't see much car traffic early in the morning.

The Tárcoles River Bridge, north of the park, draws swarms of tourists peeking over the edge at the gigantic crocodiles sunning below but also shows birds like the Mangrove Swallow, several heron and egret species, and with any luck, the Double-striped Thick-knee. For a closer look, take a mangrove boat tour along this murky river to see the Southern Lapwing, Ringed Kingfisher, Roseate Spoonbill, and American Pygmy Kingfisher.

Slightly north of the Tárcoles River Bridge are some ponds of interest where you can usually find Wood Storks and Great Egrets. And farther north, you can access the Guacimo road, which connects Route 27 to Guacalillo Beach. This long, rough road (4x4 required) contains dry forest habitat and attracts species like the Lesser Ground Cuckoo, Stripe-headed Sparrow, Orange-fronted Parakeet, White-fronted Parrot, Inca Dove, and White-lored Gnatcatcher.

7

FAMILY FUN

Costa Rica has a lot to offer if you're traveling with kids. With tons of wildlife and a variety of exciting activities, Costa Rica will keep even the busiest little ones entertained. Below we share the best itinerary for family travel. Each destination has been carefully selected with the kids in mind, while ensuring a relaxing getaway for the adults too. You should have no trouble finding family-friendly accommodations, restaurants, and activities, and we've selected routes that will show you the best of Costa Rica without having to spend too much time in the car. Finally, we've chosen destinations with safety in mind. While Costa Rica is generally very safe, like anywhere in the world, some areas are better than others. You will feel at ease taking your family to all the towns recommended.

*Only Included in
Two Week Itinerary

One Week Itinerary: La Fortuna (3 days) to Nosara (4 days). Recommended Airport: LIR. View transportation options for this itinerary on p. 143.

Two Week Itinerary: La Fortuna (4 days) to Nosara (5 days, includes day trips to Sámara and Punta Islita) to Manuel Antonio (5 days). Because the two-week itinerary ends in Manuel Antonio, the recommended airport is SJO. View transportation options for this itinerary on p. 144.

La Fortuna

One Week Itinerary: La Fortuna – Days 1-3

Two Week Itinerary: La Fortuna – Days 1-4

The charming town of La Fortuna in the rolling hills of northwestern Costa Rica is the perfect place to start your family holiday. Located a few hours from the international airports (around 3 hours from Liberia and 3-4 hours from San José), this town is situated around a beautiful central park and garden with the mighty Arenal Volcano in the backdrop. Here, you'll find lots of kid-friendly activities like wildlife watching, rainforest night tours, and hanging bridges. Though the downtown is modest in size, it features plenty of restaurants from upscale eateries to casual cafés and pizzerias that will please the pickiest of palates. There are even ice-cream shops and a candy store. Accommodations vary widely from luxury resorts with hot-spring pools to treehouses in the jungle and eco-lodges with volcano views.

Transportation Tip: Although there are other options, a rental car may be the most economical choice for this itinerary given the cost for 3 or more people to take a shuttle or small plane between destinations. See the Transportation Guide (p. 143) for more information.

The Highlight

The highlight for families in La Fortuna is a night walk at a local nature reserve. Just after sunset, you'll creep along flat trails by the glow of a flashlight to spy rainforest creatures that only come out after dark. With the help of a guide, you'll spot frogs like the red-eyed tree frog, see-through glass frog, or tiny green-and-black poison dart frog. Other kinds of wildlife also can be seen during these walks, including caimans, armadillos, sloths, snakes, lizards, and a variety of intriguing insects like leaf-cutter ants and stick bugs.

A couple of the best places to do a night walk are **Arenal Oasis** (p. 162), an eco-lodge with a small refuge, and **EcoCentro Danaus Ecological Reserve** (p. 162). Both have experienced guides who will teach you a lot about the animals you discover. What's great about these tours is that you're guaranteed to see wildlife—something that doesn't always happen on day hikes. Not only will you have the help of your guide, but these reserves have been selectively landscaped and carefully designed around ponds and other native habitat to attract the most wildlife.

Frog eggs hidden under a leaf

Other Activities and Attractions

When in La Fortuna, Arenal Volcano is a must-see, but if you have young children, don't feel like you have to go hiking to see it. This cone-shaped giant is 5,437 feet (1,633 meters) tall and can be seen from all around town. If you would like to hike, a couple of places with trails that aren't too difficult are **Arenal Volcano National Park** (p. 162) and the **Arenal Observatory** (p. 162). The Observatory also has a nice deck outside its restaurant where you can conveniently take in the close-up view.

While it doesn't enjoy volcano views from the trails, another great place for family nature discovery is the

Arenal Hanging Bridges (p. 163). Here, you can spend a couple of hours exploring the rainforest canopy along 1.25 km (2 miles) of mostly flat, well-maintained trails and secure hanging bridges. Many types of birds are typically spotted at the Arenal Hanging Bridges, but with the help of a guide, you're likely to see lots more like snakes camouflaged around trees, monkeys, and white-nosed coati, a small mammal that resembles a raccoon.

Although we recommend visiting a wildlife center later on in your trip in Nosara, try to fit in a visit to **Proyecto Asis** (p. 163) too. Proyecto Asis, located outside La Fortuna in Ciudad Quesada, offers a couple of different tours, but all will teach the kids about conservation and have them within arm's reach of wildlife like monkeys, coatis, parrots, and toucans. The longer, 3.5 hour volunteering tour includes the chance to care for and feed the animals. *Reservations required.*

La Fortuna has lots of choices for hot springs, but your best bet for the family is probably the **Baldi Resort** (p. 162). Spend the day soaking in the natural pools and have a cocktail at the swim-up bar, while the kids play in the smaller pools and on waterslides in the children's area.

Other family-friendly things to do include kayaking on Lake Arenal for great volcano views, zip lining, the **Rainforest Chocolate tour** (p. 163), and **La Fortuna Waterfall** (p. 163). Note that to get to La Fortuna Waterfall, you can either take a horseback tour or access it from the visitors center. From the visitors center, you have to walk down around 500 steps. They are well maintained, but it can be a tough hike back up for older people and very young children. **Tip:** The rocks around the falls can get slippery so take water shoes for the kids if you have them.

Nosara

One Week Itinerary: Nosara – Days 4-7

Two Week Itinerary: Nosara – Days 5-9

After La Fortuna, head to Guanacaste Province for some time at the beach. Nosara is located about 4-5 hours from La Fortuna in a remote area of the central Nicoya Peninsula. This makes it slightly difficult to get to, but that's all part of the appeal. The raw jungle and rough roads will make it feel like you're a world away even though there are many amenities nearby. **Tip:** If you need to break up the drive, stop for a couple of hours for a swim at the majestic **Llanos de Cortéz Waterfall** (p. 160), right off the highway near Bagaces. Secure parking is available and it is just a quick five-minute walk to reach the falls.

Once you arrive in Nosara, you'll see that this laid-back town is very spread out and best explored with a rental car (four-wheel drive recommended). The town is divided into different sections, with the main areas being closest to Playa Pelada, a beach to the north, and Playa Guiones, a beach to the south. Guiones houses the majority of businesses, but if you have a car, everything is within a short drive. For restaurants, Nosara offers cuisine from all over the world with many kid-friendly options. You can find authentic Italian pizza and pasta, tacos, sandwiches, burgers, fresh fish, and even smoothies and homemade gelato. Accommodations are numerous and vary from yoga and surf retreats to stylish hotels near the beach and lodges set privately in the hills. A good option for families for this leg of the trip is a vacation rental. With a large expat community, there are lots of houses for rent by the day or week, many of which feature pools and ocean views. And if you're lucky, you'll have monkeys right in your backyard.

The Highlight

The Nosara Wildlife Center will not only get the whole family up close to monkeys but will also teach you about the issues affecting Costa Rica's wildlife. The center is made up of two groups, the Refuge for Wildlife and Sibu Sanctuary. Both are dedicated to rescuing and rehabilitating injured animals, most commonly howler monkeys, which are sometimes injured because of uninsulated power lines. The wonderful people at the centers take these animals in, treat them, and rehabilitate them in spacious jungle enclosures in the hopes of releasing them back into the wild.

The two organizations have different locations and goals. The **Refuge for Wildlife** (p. 168) focuses on providing immediate and long-term medical attention, while **Sibu Sanctuary** (p. 168) gets the monkeys ready for reintroduction into the wild once they have received medical care. Visiting either facility is an unforgettable experience. *Advanced reservations required. Minimum age to visit Refuge for Wildlife is 7 years (10 years and up recommended). Sibu Sanctuary has no minimum age requirements and is better for younger children. See the Activities Guide (p. 168) for more information.*

Other Activities and Attractions

If your timing is right, your family could witness a spectacle of nature called an *arribada*, where olive ridley sea turtles come to shore in mass numbers to lay their eggs. The turtles nest at Playa Ostional, just north of Nosara, year-round but most frequently during the rainy season (peak times: August to December). Tours are either at night (by the light of a flashlight) or very early in the morning. Be sure to ask around town if there are any signs of an *arribada*. Word of them spreads quickly and you'll want to book a guide fast.

Another great activity in Nosara for the family is **horseback riding** (p. 168). On a relaxing ride through town, you'll get to explore the surrounding jungle and beach, learning more about the area from a knowledgeable local. A few tour operators in Nosara have horses that are more docile and good for beginner riders so be sure to inquire when booking.

To explore some of the area's tranquil rivers, arrange a **kayak or stand-up paddleboard tour** (p. 168) up the Río Nosara or Río Montaña. Paddling quietly through calm water, you'll be able to sneak up on lots of birds and animals hidden in the thick forest and mangroves.

For swimming, many of the beaches in Costa Rica have rough water, and Nosara, which is known for surfing, is no exception. Conditions change constantly but all the area beaches experience large waves and riptides. The best place for kids is Playa Pelada, which has a sheltered cove and a rock formation that locals call the blow hole because it shoots water high into the air with incoming waves.

The blow hole at Playa Pelada

A great way to explore the nearby mountains, especially with older kids, is on an ATV or off-road Tomcar tour. Other things to do in the area include a climbing wall, skate park, mini-golf course, or taking a zip-line tour or surf lesson.

Sámara and Punta Islita
(Day Trips from Nosara)

One Week Itinerary: Omitted from one-week itinerary.

Two Week Itinerary: Visit Sámara and Punta Islita on day trips from Nosara.

Beach Day in Sámara: The two-week vacationer can explore more of the area with a day trip to the small town of Sámara. Located about a half hour to the south, Sámara is the perfect place for a beach day with the kids because it enjoys relatively calm water due to a protected reef. The main town of Sámara is adjacent to the beach, so after you've had enough swimming and sandcastle-making, you can walk right to shops and souvenir stands or grab lunch at one of the beach bars.

Punta Islita: The **Ara Project** (p. 171) is a macaw parrot breeding and release center near the village of Punta Islita, about 1.5 hours south of Nosara. Scarlet and Great Green Macaws have become endangered in Costa Rica due to habitat loss and the illegal pet trade, and this organization is doing amazing work toward reintroducing the species. On this little-known tour, you'll learn about these beautiful birds and have the unique opportunity to see almost 100 Scarlet Macaws, many flying free right overhead.

On your visit to Punta Islita, be sure to take a drive past the center of town along the mountainous coastline

for great ocean views. It is also worth a quick stop at
Museo Islita (p. 171), a small open-air contemporary art
museum near the soccer field in town, which features
artwork from local Costa Ricans. **Tip:** Make sure you have
a four-wheel-drive vehicle for this trip as some of the
roads between Sámara and Punta Islita are rough dirt and
mountainous.

Manuel Antonio

One Week Itinerary: Omitted. Trip ends in Nosara.

Two Week Itinerary: Manuel Antonio – Days 10-14

After you've explored Guanacaste Province, spend the
remainder of your two weeks in the lush rainforest of the
central Pacific coast. Outside the Nosara area, the road
turns from bumpy dirt to smooth highway and along the
way, you'll cross the beautiful Tempisque River and enjoy
sweeping views of the Gulf of Nicoya. To break up the 5-
hour drive, stop at the Tárcoles River just before the town
of Jacó. Here, you can walk along the bridge and show the
kids, at a safe distance, the giant crocodiles that live below.

Once you arrive in Manuel Antonio, you'll traverse up a
hill, passing the many businesses that line the main drag.
Although Manuel Antonio is more developed, much of the
land has been preserved so there is still plenty of rainforest.
What makes Manuel Antonio a top destination for families
is the sheer number of restaurants, hotels, activities, and
attractions all in one place. Lodging ranges from luxury
bungalows and fully equipped vacation rentals to affordable
hotels, many of which cater specifically to families. The
multitude of restaurants makes it easy to find something for
everyone too. Most of the restaurants are also open air so
more casual and perfect for young children.

Tip: Manuel Antonio is easily manageable without a car. If you rented a car for the first part of your trip, you could drop it off in Manuel Antonio/Quepos after driving from Nosara and get around locally by taxi or the bus.

The Highlight

The main draw in Manuel Antonio for families is the chance to get up close and personal with wild monkeys. Sure you'll see howler monkeys in Nosara, but in Manuel Antonio, it is common to see monkeys on the grounds of hotels or swinging in the trees outside restaurants. Three species are endemic to Manuel Antonio: howler monkeys, white-faced capuchin monkeys, and squirrel monkeys. Notably, Manuel Antonio is one of the only places in Costa Rica where you can see the endangered gray-crowned squirrel monkey. **Tip:** Make sure to explain to the kids that it is best not to feed the monkeys. Although many people do, the bacteria on human hands can harm the monkeys' delicate digestive systems and even cause death.

Activities and Attractions

Another reason Manuel Antonio is so good for families is that it has a national park right in town. **Manuel Antonio National Park** (p. 165) is located at the very end of the road near the beach. It has five trails that vary in difficulty, but the main trail is flat and wide (more like a road) and not too long, so perfect for younger children. Inside the park, you can easily spot all different kinds of wildlife like raccoons, sloths, hermit crabs, monkeys, iguanas, and butterflies. Be sure to pack a lunch and your swimsuits, because unlike the main beach in Manuel Antonio, which has rough surf, there is a beautiful protected cove inside the park. Playa Manuel Antonio, just a short walk from the park entrance, is perfect for swimming and has bathrooms, outdoor showers, changing rooms, and a few picnic tables so you can make a day of it.

Tip: Arrive early, close to when the park opens, to see the most wildlife and avoid the crowds. Manuel Antonio is the busiest park in Costa Rica, and lines start forming to get in around 9:00 a.m. during the busy season (December through April). *Closed Mondays during the low season (July 1 – Nov. 30).*

For another great beach for the kids, head to **Playa Biesanz** on the road to Punta Quepos. This secluded cove enjoys calm water for swimming and has plenty of shade so is another nice place to spend the day. There aren't any amenities nearby, so be sure to stock up on snacks at one of the small grocery stores in town and take everything you need. Playa Biesanz is not marked so refer to the Activities Guide (p. 165) at the end of the book for guidance on getting there.

From Manuel Antonio, you can book almost any tour imaginable to fill the rest of your five days. If you want more fun on the water, consider a **catamaran excursion** (p. 164). Several companies offer these tours, which will take you offshore around Manuel Antonio's beautiful coast and rocky islands. A stop in one of the calmer coves will give you a chance to swim or snorkel, and certain boats even have fun slides to keep the kids entertained while you relax with a cold drink.

Zip lining (p. 165) is another favorite family activity where, with a helmet and harness, you'll fly weightlessly through the treetops along a secure steel cable. Manuel Antonio has several operators offering these tours. Some combine the zip lining with education to teach you more about nature and the forest, while others focus on the rush, letting you soar head first like superheroes. Age restrictions vary by company (generally starting at ages 4 or 5) so be sure to inquire before booking.

Although you will have seen wildlife centers elsewhere during your trip, there is another really special one just outside Manuel Antonio. **Kids Saving the Rainforest** (p. 164) was originally started by a couple of forward-thinking kids on a mission to protect the rainforest. Like those kids, the center has grown over the years and now KSTR, along with its newest project, the Sloth Institute, rehabilitates and releases animals that have been injured in the wild or captured in the illegal pet trade. You can see some of these animals by visiting the KSTR Sanctuary near Quepos.

Other fun family activities are horseback tours to waterfalls, kayaking or boat trips through the mangroves at **Isla Damas** (p. 164), white-water rafting, canyoning (rappelling down waterfalls), four-wheeling, stand-up paddleboarding, and Segway tours.

8

ECO-TREKKING

Costa Rica may look small on a map but don't let that fool you. With steamy tropical rainforest, arid dry forest, misty cloud forest, and seaside mangroves, Costa Rica hosts an impressively diverse geography. And with one of the most extensive park systems in the world, accessing these areas is safe and easy. Below we share an itinerary for eco-trekking in Costa Rica that will have you hiking through dense rainforest and cloud forest, discovering active volcanos, and admiring majestic waterfalls.

One Week Itinerary: La Fortuna (4 days, includes day trip to Río Celeste Waterfall) to Monteverde (3 days). Recommended Airport: SJO or LIR. View transportation options for this itinerary on p. 146.

Two Week Itinerary: La Fortuna (4 days, includes day trip to Río Celeste Waterfall) to Monteverde (3 days) to Southern Zone (4 days) to Drake Bay (3 days). Recommended Airport: SJO. View transportation options for this itinerary on p. 147.

La Fortuna

One Week Itinerary: La Fortuna – Days 1-4

Two Week Itinerary: La Fortuna – Days 1-4

Start your eco-trekking experience in the mountains of northwestern Costa Rica with a visit to the small town of La Fortuna. La Fortuna has an abundance of outdoor activities for the eco-trekker, including volcanos, adventure tours, and lots of opportunities for hiking and wildlife viewing. The area offers a range of lodging for all budgets, many of which are eco-lodges with their own trails on-site. If you don't rent a car, opt to stay in the very walkable downtown and arrange tours through one of the many operators. Those with a car can stay outside the center of town on the road that leads to Arenal Volcano and goes around Lake Arenal. This area is surrounded by rainforest and much more secluded.

Tip: For the two-week itinerary, the most convenient airport is San José's SJO, while for the one-week itinerary, either San José or Liberia are suitable as drive times are similar. For more information, see the Transportation Guide (p. 146) for this itinerary.

The Highlight

The eco-trekking highlight of La Fortuna is the challenging hike to **Cerro Chato** (p. 162), a dormant volcano with a stunning emerald-green crater lake. Cerro Chato is located along the same ridge as Arenal Volcano and can be accessed from either the Arenal Observatory or the Green Lagoon Lodge. From either location, the approximately 2-hour trek in each direction is moderate to difficult and not recommended for young children. Those reaching the summit (1,140 meters or 3,740 feet) will be rewarded with a view of the shimmering crater lake below. As a bonus, if you can negotiate the steep, slippery climb down into the crater, you can cool off with a swim.

Tip: Be sure to wear hiking boots and clothes you don't mind getting muddy; trekking polls would be useful as well for the steep climb. Also take plenty of water as conditions are typically hot and humid.

The crater lake at Cerro Chato

Other Activities and Attractions

Of course, a trekking experience in La Fortuna wouldn't be complete without a visit to Arenal Volcano. Although Arenal is no longer spewing orange lava, this 1,633 meter (5,437 foot) tall, perfectly cone-shaped volcano is still a must-see. Hiking to the top of this active giant is not permitted for safety reasons, but you can still get a closer look. **Tip:** The volcano is sometimes covered in clouds so for best visibility, visit during the dry season of December to April.

The most popular access point is **Arenal Volcano National Park** (p. 162). This park has 6 km (3.75 miles) of paths that are fairly flat and appropriate for most abilities. From viewpoints, you will get a close-up of the volcano's western face and see Costa Rica's largest lake, Lake Arenal, in the distance. **Arenal 1968** (p. 162), a private reserve located next to the park, offers 8 km (5 miles) of slightly more difficult trails passing viewpoints and former lava fields from the last big eruption in 1968. Finally, the **Arenal Observatory** (p. 162) has the largest network of trails and, as noted above, is also an access point to Cerro

Chato. The Observatory has spectacular volcano views, excellent bird-watching, a waterfall, and a hanging bridge.

Because of the varied topography and mixture of habitats around Arenal Volcano, you're likely to see many types of mammals as well as resident and migratory birds. Commonly spotted mammals are white-nosed coati, mantled howler and white-faced capuchin monkeys, and for birds, the Magpie Jay, Great Curassow, and Gray-headed Chachalaca.

Once you've had your fill of hiking, take in some of the area's other unique sights. **La Fortuna Waterfall** (p. 163) plummets 70 meters (230 feet) into a deep pool surrounded by moss-covered rocks and plants. This is a popular attraction, now complete with a visitors center, but is still worth a trip. Access to the falls is via a set of 500 steep, but well maintained, steps. Arrive early to avoid the crowds.

The area's **hot springs** (p. 162) are another attraction you won't find in many places in Costa Rica. Resorts offer day passes, but you can also soothe your aching muscles in one of the steaming rivers for free near the Tabacon Resort. Other activities in the La Fortuna area for the eco-trekker include zip lining, **white-water rafting** (p. 164), **canyoning** (rappelling down waterfalls) (p. 162), and the **Venado Caves** (p. 164).

Río Celeste Waterfall
(Day Trip from La Fortuna)

One Week Itinerary: Visit Río Celeste Waterfall on day trip from La Fortuna.

Two Week Itinerary: Visit Río Celeste Waterfall on day trip from La Fortuna.

Not too far from La Fortuna is one of Costa Rica's most amazing waterfalls. Located a couple of hours to the

northwest, **Tenorio Volcano National Park** (p. 163) is
one of the least touristy areas of the country. Although
there aren't too many attractions, the vast farmland, rolling
hills, and stunning Celeste River and Waterfall make it well
worth the full day trip from La Fortuna.

Tenorio Volcano National Park's moderately difficult,
often muddy, trail meanders through the rainforest,
passing several points of interest along the way. You'll see
bubbling *aguas termales* (hot springs) and *teñideros*, the point
where volcanic minerals mix to turn the river from crystal
clear to baby blue. But the main attraction is the Río
Celeste Waterfall. Like La Fortuna Waterfall, you have to
walk down a set of steep steps (250) to reach the Río
Celeste Waterfall, but it is an unforgettable experience to
see the bright blue ribbon of water, which looks like it
came straight out of a fairytale.

Tip: Plan your visit during the dry season of December
to April and around rainstorms, if possible. Rain can cloud
the water and dull the turquoise effect. Note: Swimming at
the waterfall is no longer permitted.

Monteverde

One Week Itinerary: Monteverde – Days 5-7

Two Week Itinerary: Monteverde – Days 5-7

After discovering the volcanos of La Fortuna, head over to
the rugged Cordillera de Tilarán Mountains to experience a
completely different life zone: the cloud forest. Located just
a few hours from La Fortuna, the Quaker-established
Monteverde and neighboring Santa Elena host many
accommodations, restaurants, and other tourist amenities.
Santa Elena has a small downtown with restaurants, cafés,
and budget-friendly hotels, while Monteverde is more spread

out, with businesses stretching the length of the road leading to the Monteverde Cloud Forest Reserve. Eco-lodges and small inns tucked into the forest are available in both towns.

Tip: If you're driving yourself, get a rental car with four-wheel drive as the roads to Monteverde are rough dirt. Read our Transportation Guide (p. 146) for more details and alternative options.

The Highlight

The main eco-trekking attraction in Monteverde is the cloud forest, a unique ecosystem located at the Continental Divide where the Atlantic and Pacific slopes converge. The near-constant, misty cloud cover here is unlike anything you've ever seen before. While hundreds of different types of birds and other animals live in this biologically rich jungle, it can be difficult to spot them in the thick cover. Hiring a guide in one of the nearby reserves is the best way to see the most in a short time while learning a lot about the different species.

Of the main reserves, the most popular is the **Monteverde Cloud Forest Reserve** (p. 167), which boasts eight trails totaling 13 km (8 miles), a 100 meter (325 foot) long hanging bridge, and a small waterfall. Because Monteverde is the most popular reserve, it tends to be the busiest. The higher elevation **Santa Elena Cloud Forest Reserve** (p. 167) and the **Children's Eternal Rainforest** (p. 166) both offer a similar experience to the Monteverde Reserve and tend to see less foot traffic. The Bajo del Tigre entrance, not far from downtown Santa Elena, is the easiest way to access the expansive Children's Eternal Rainforest. The Santa Elena Reserve can be accessed via the ranger station on the northeast side of town.

Another great way to explore the cloud forest is by hanging bridge. A visit to **Selvatura** (p. 167) or **Sky Adventures** (p. 167) will have you high up in the canopy, giving you a closer view of birds and certain types of wildlife that can be difficult to spot from the ground like the rare Resplendent Quetzal.

Tip: The cloud forest is a bit cooler (averaging 19°C or 66°F) and often rainy so be sure to wear pants, shirts for layering, and a raincoat.

Other Activities and Attractions

Once you've explored the cloud forest on foot, get a bird's-eye view on a **canopy zip-line tour** (p. 168). Monteverde is one of the best places in Costa Rica for these tours because of its lush greenery and glorious mountains. You'll find people of all ages, from four to 74, strapping on a helmet and harness for the chance to glide weightlessly above the tree line. Several operators offer tours, with runs ranging from a comfortable 20 meters (66 feet) to a thrilling 1,590 meters (5,217 feet).

If you need to refuel after all this adventure, take a coffee tour. Several producers in the area will show you around their facility and teach you what goes into making the perfect cup of high-altitude java. **El Trapiche** (p. 166) and **Don Juan** (p. 166) each offer a combination coffee-sugarcane-chocolate tour, or for a more personal experience, visit **El Cafetal** (p. 166) to hear the perspectives of a smaller organic grower.

Other activities in Monteverde that may interest the eco-trekker are horseback riding, canyoning, and for the bird lover, the **Hummingbird Gallery** (p. 167) near the Monteverde Cloud Forest Reserve.

Southern Zone

One Week Itinerary: Omitted. Trip ends in Monteverde.

Two Week Itinerary: Southern Zone – Days 8-11

After you've explored the mountains of northwestern Costa Rica, the two-week vacationer will head south from Monteverde to the Southern Zone (4-5 hours) for more nature and hiking. This rainforest-covered region includes the beaches of the southern Pacific coast and stretches into the steep forested mountains.

The best way to access this spread-out area is from the small coastal towns of Dominical or Uvita. Dominical is a laid-back surfer town about 45 minutes south of Manuel Antonio. It isn't as developed as the popular resort town of Manuel Antonio but still has a number of casual restaurants and bars along the main strip near the beach. Uvita, located 15 minutes south of Dominical, is another small town that has some notable attractions, including a national marine park and beautiful beaches as well as a modest selection of restaurants and shops. While both Uvita and Dominical have a handful of choices for basic lodging near the beach, those looking for bed and breakfasts, eco-lodges, luxury villas, and vacation rentals should head to the surrounding hills.

Tip: Activities and amenities in the Southern Zone are very spread out so a rental car (with four-wheel drive) is recommended for this leg of the trip.

The Highlight

Located about 1.5 hours from Dominical is **Cerro Chirripó** (p. 158), the eco-trekking highlight of the Southern Zone. This is Costa Rica's tallest mountain at 3,820 meters (12,533 feet), and the steep, 16 km (10 mile) hike to the peak is not for everyone. Starting from the base near the village of San Gerardo de Rivas, this hike requires at least two days with an overnight stay at the ranger station below the summit. A lot of planning and work goes into this trek. You need an entrance ticket from the ranger station, best reserved well in advance, and cold-weather gear as temperatures sometimes reach near

freezing at night due to the altitude. But for the serious
trekker, this is one of the most rewarding hikes in Costa
Rica. With a little luck (and not too many clouds), it is
possible to see both the Caribbean Sea and the Pacific
Ocean from the summit.

Tip: If you want more time to explore Cerro Chirripó's
magnificent mountains, book a night or two in one of the
remote towns near the ranger station like San Gerardo de
Rivas. Or to be closer to amenities, stay in the small city of
San Isidro del General, which is only 19 km (12 miles)
from Chirripó.

For a taste of Chirripó without the days of hiking, right
near the base of the mountain is **Cloudbridge Nature
Reserve** (p. 158). This 283 hectare (700 acre) private
reserve has an extensive trail system with waterfalls,
flowering gardens, and a hanging bridge and covered
bridge. Although not as high in altitude, the diverse cloud
forest habitat provides a challenging hike and is home to
tons of birds and other wildlife.

Clouds rolling in at Cloudbridge Nature Reserve

Other Activities and Attractions

One of the most spectacular waterfalls in Costa Rica are the Nauyaca located in the mountains about 20 minutes from Dominical. The **Nauyaca Waterfalls** (p. 158) have two levels, an upper falls that tumble 43 meters (140 feet) and a smaller, 18 meter (60 foot) lower falls that cascade into an oversized pool perfect for swimming. You can reach the Nauyaca via a fairly easy 4 km (2.5 mile) long hike or on a horseback tour.

Right off the main highway in Dominical and Uvita, you'll find more great hiking through verdant tropical rainforest where you may spot white-faced monkeys, collared peccaries, white-nosed coati, and exotic birds like toucans, aracaris, and parrots. **Hacienda Barú Wildlife Refuge** (p. 158) near Dominical is a great day-hiking option for all levels and is a prime spot for birding. A lesser known reserve where you may see more wildlife due to a lack of foot traffic is **Tesoro Escondido Reserve** (p. 159) in Playa Hermosa, just north of Uvita.

To cool off after hiking, head to the beaches of the Southern Zone, some of the most beautiful in the country. The main beach in Uvita, Playa Uvita, is part of one of Costa Rica's only marine parks. **Marino Ballena National Park** (Whale Marine National Park) (p. 158) got its name from the huge, naturally occurring whale-tail-shaped sandbar, which can be walked at low tide, and also for the humpback whales, which migrate through the area twice a year to breed and rear young. If you're visiting from mid-July to October or December to March, consider taking a **whale-watching tour** (p. 159) to see these mystical giants passing through.

Drake Bay

One Week Itinerary: Omitted. Trip ends in Monteverde.

Two Week Itinerary: Drake Bay – Days 12-14

The Southern Zone will give you a taste of Costa Rica's tropical forests, but for the full experience, two-week trekkers won't want to miss Drake Bay. This quiet village is located in the remote Osa Peninsula in the middle of the pristine jungle. Here, roads feel more like trails, monkeys outnumber people, and you'll find the most rugged trekking in the entire country.

From the Southern Zone, you'll travel about an hour south along nicely paved highway to Sierpe. At the river in town, you'll grab a speedboat ride through mangroves, landing in the village of Drake after a short trip down the coast. Note: Although driving to Drake Bay is possible, it is not recommended due to multiple river crossings and rough roads. With only one main road in town, you can easily get around on foot like most locals do. After your time in Drake Bay, we recommend taking a small plane directly to San José to save time. For other transportation options, refer to the Transportation Guide (p. 148).

Despite being difficult to access, Drake Bay offers travelers plenty of amenities. Lodging ranges from boutique hotels and small resorts to inexpensive cabins and tent camps. Due to the remote nature of this destination and because there are few restaurants in town, most hotels offer packages that include meals and sometimes tours.

The Highlight

The eco-trekker comes to Drake Bay for **Corcovado National Park** (p. 159), a 417 sq km (161 sq mile) mass of jungle known across the globe for its rich biodiversity. All four types of monkeys found in Costa Rica live in the park as well as sloths, Scarlet Macaw parrots, peccaries, giant Baird's tapir, and even pumas and jaguars. While much of this huge protected tract of wild rainforest is inaccessible, trekkers can explore the trails through the four ranger stations. For those up for a multi-day excursion, you can hike all day and camp overnight at the stations. Book well in advance to reserve a spot during peak seasons (December through April). Note: Park rangers periodically close parts of the park, and the most challenging section of the trail system, the 25 km (16 mile) stretch from San Pedrillo to Sirena, was closed as of the time of this writing. Check with park rangers or a guide for the most up-to-date information.

Day-trippers can jump on a boat from Drake Bay to San Pedrillo Ranger Station or the more distant Sirena Ranger Station for a shorter trek and some great wildlife exploring.

As of 2014, a licensed guide is required to visit the park, both for day trips and overnights. Guides are available through tour operators in Drake Bay. See the Activities Guide (p. 159) for more information.

Other Activities and Attractions

Outside the park limits, a great option for hiking is the remote path from Drake Bay to a beach called Playa San Josecito. This long but beautiful hike follows the jungle-backed coastline, crossing an emerald-green river by suspension bridge and passing many desolate beaches. Shortly before arriving at Playa San Josecito, you'll have to wade across a small river, the Río Claro. If the tide is high, a friendly local can help you cross by boat for a small fee. Leave early for this full-day excursion and take some snorkel gear as the beach has a protected reef right offshore.

The peaceful village of Drake Bay doesn't have much going on at night, but one fun activity is a **night hike** (p. 160). You can do these tours all around Costa Rica, but nowhere else has Drake Bay's intriguing array of insects, reptiles, and amphibians. Only a few operators offer tours so be sure to book through your hotel in advance.

Other activities in Drake Bay that may interest the eco-trekker are snorkel and dive tours off the marine-rich **Caño Island** (p. 159), dolphin and whale watching, mangrove tours, kayaking, and river float trips.

9

GUANACASTE BEACHES

The shores of Costa Rica's Guanacaste Province are known worldwide for their stunning beauty. Dubbed the Gold Coast, this area has countless postcard-worthy beaches like the white sand Playa Flamingo, the shell-filled Playa Conchal, and the hidden Playa Avellanas. Be sure to stock up on the sunscreen because this itinerary will have you beach-hopping all around Costa Rica's northern Pacific coast. From the drier plains to the lush rainforest, we highlight the best destinations for relaxing, swimming, and beachside lounging. We also provide information on area activities and attractions for when you want to step off the sand and explore.

One Week Itinerary: Tamarindo/Flamingo (7 days). Recommended Airport: LIR. View transportation options for this itinerary on p. 150.

Two Week Itinerary: Tamarindo/Flamingo (7 days) to Sámara (7 days). Recommended Airport: LIR. View transportation options for this itinerary on p. 150.

Tamarindo/Flamingo

One Week Itinerary: Tamarindo or Flamingo – Days 1-7

Two Week Itinerary: Tamarindo or Flamingo – Days 1-7

Because many of Guanacaste's beaches are clustered within a small geographic area, they can easily be explored from one centrally located town. Opt to stay in either Tamarindo or Flamingo and use it as a jumping-off point to visit other areas on day trips. Both towns make a great home base. They each have their own beautiful beach and plenty of amenities, and are just a short drive to other attractions. These locations are also close to Liberia International Airport (about 1 hour), making them easy to reach even with later arrivals.

Transportation Tip: A rental car is recommended for this itinerary so that you have flexibility to explore the lesser-known beaches to the north and south. Rental cars are available at the airport in Liberia. For more information, see the Transportation Guide (p. 150).

Of the two destinations, the surfer town of Tamarindo is more built up, with a downtown near the beach that has many hotels, restaurants, bars, and shops. While still hanging on to its laid-back roots, Tamarindo is one of the most developed areas of Costa Rica and even has a few mid-rise condos. If you stay in town, everything will be within walking distance, including the beach. Although many people love Tamarindo for its pure convenience, variety of upscale eateries, and nightlife, some visitors find it too busy and touristy, especially during peak travel months (December through April).

If you're seeking a more relaxed pace, consider Flamingo. Flamingo is an upscale destination just north of Tamarindo with small beach clubs, condos, and vacation rentals all set around a lovely white sand beach. Due to its location on a peninsula, Flamingo has gorgeous ocean views, and many accommodations are set in the hills to take advantage. The community of Flamingo is on the smaller side, but there is still a good selection of restaurants, and activities can be easily arranged.

Tip: Northwestern Guanacaste is the driest region in Costa Rica. By the end of Costa Rica's "summer" (April), the landscape is often dry and brown due to lack of water. If you'd rather see everything lush and green, visit during the beginning of the dry season in December/January or the beginning of the rainy season in June.

The Highlight

Costa Rica has hundreds of beautiful beaches along its nearly 1,800 km (1,100 miles) of coastline, but one of the most spectacular is Playa Conchal. Known for its sand made of tiny crushed seashells, Playa Conchal is situated between two rocky points and has aquamarine water with picturesque islets just offshore. Not only is the beach stunningly beautiful, but the water is calm due to its location in a protected cove. This makes Playa Conchal a great destination for swimming, snorkeling, or just taking in the view from your beach chair.

The northern end of beautiful Playa Conchal

Playa Conchal doesn't have any roads leading directly to it so the best means of access is through the town of Brasilito. Park your car in Brasilito and walk 10 minutes south along the shore. Although it is possible to drive, driving on the beach is illegal in Costa Rica and can harm the area's delicate ecosystem. Access to Playa Conchal is also available for guests of the Westin, a large oceanfront resort.

Horseback tours, jet skis, kayaks, and snorkeling equipment are all available at Playa Conchal. The beach doesn't have any restaurants, aside from those at the private Westin Resort, but if you get hungry, just head back to Brasilito. This small fishing village has a few restaurants right on the beach, serving up the best local catch.

Day Trips to Other Nearby Beaches

You won't find any other beaches in Guanacaste with sand made of shells, but there are plenty more beautiful spots to explore.

Playa Grande: A short drive or boat ride across the river mouth from Tamarindo is Playa Grande, a much less crowded beach best known for its big waves. Watch the expert surfers in action from the light tan sand or stroll up the coast to explore tide pools. The coastline stretches for miles to the north past several rocky points, which lead to other secluded beaches like the black sand Playa Carbón. There isn't much shade, but the small community of Playa Grande has a few restaurants where you can rest up and grab a bite to eat. This beach is also an important nesting site for leatherback sea turtles (see Activities and Attractions below for more details).

Playa Brasilito: If you're looking for another private beach, try the cove at the northern end of Playa Brasilito. This little-known spot outside town is quiet and just as beautiful as the nearby Playa Flamingo, but sees much fewer visitors. The beach has offshore rock formations, calm azure waters, and plenty of space to kick back and relax. Be sure to take whatever refreshments you'll need, as once you get out of the small center of Brasilito, there are no amenities. For access, look for the dirt road at the sharp curve just after the center of town and follow it to the end.

Playa Penca: From Playa Brasilito, it is worth a 10 minute trip up the coast to see Playa Penca in the small town of Potrero. This secluded cove has a light sandy beach and alluring blue water. Grab some shade under the oversized strangler fig tree near the entrance if you can, as this beach doesn't have much vegetation. Playa Penca is accessible via a short drive down a bumpy dirt road. Look for the small sign off the main street in the center of Potrero.

Playa Avellanas: Once you've explored the beaches to the north, head south on another day trip to discover a couple of more off-the-beaten-path spots. About 30 minutes south of Tamarindo is Playa Avellanas. Driving along bumpy dirt roads and through rural communities to get there, you will be pleasantly surprised when you finally arrive at this super chill beach. The main gathering point (and parking area) is Lola's, a fun beach bar and restaurant with a resident pig. Here, surfers and families spend the day frolicking in the waves or snoozing in the shade of palm trees.

Playa Negra: This quiet surfing beach just south of Playa Avellanas is even more remote with only a few surf camps and a very small town center, which hosts a handful of hotels and restaurants. Along the salt and pepper sand, there are some beautiful tide pools and rock outcroppings. Playa Negra also has a tiki-hut-style restaurant where you can stop for a frosty Imperial (the national beer of Costa Rica) or casual meal.

Activities and Attractions

Aside from the beach, one of the main reasons visitors come to northern Guanacaste is to surf. Tamarindo and its surrounding sands attract surfing pros and newbies alike with its varying breaks up and down the coast. Grab a lesson at one of the many schools in town or rent a board to hone your skills. For lots more on surfing in the Tamarindo area, check out the Surfing chapter (p. 41).

To observe an amazing spectacle of nature, head to **Las Baulas National Marine Park** (p. 172) in Playa Grande. Here, turtle watching is possible between the months of November and March. Though you'll need a little luck to have your visit coincide with a nesting event, don't pass up the chance to see giant leatherback turtles come to shore to lay their eggs. Guided night tours are available through the ranger station in Playa Grande.

For a daytime activity, the peaceful mangroves at the nearby **Tamarindo Estuary** (p. 172) are rich in wildlife like howler monkeys, crocodiles, and a variety of birds. Boat and kayak tours are both available. For something farther from the beach, walk the trails at the volcanic **Rincon de la Vieja National Park** (p. 160), about 2 hours from Tamarindo. At this park, you will see bubbling mud pots, steaming fumaroles, and a seasonal waterfall, all while hiking through some thick forest around the base of an active volcano. Afterwards, hit up one of the area spas for a treatment with the mineral-rich mud.

Other popular activities around Tamarindo and Playa Flamingo include in-shore and deep-sea sportfishing, diving and snorkeling around the area's many reefs, kayaking, stand-up paddleboarding, sunset cruises, and whale-watching tours. For adventure by land, there is golf as well as ATV and zip-line tours.

Sámara

One Week Itinerary: Omitted. Trip ends in Tamarindo/Flamingo.

Two Week Itinerary: Sámara – Days 8-14

If you're continuing on for another week, shake out your towel and head to the beautiful beaches of the central Nicoya Peninsula. Located about two hours south of Tamarindo, the central Nicoya will show you a lush environment with a more jungle-like feel than you will have experienced in the arid north. You will also notice as you drive farther south that the peninsula becomes less developed, the wildlife more plentiful, and many of the roads more rugged. **Tip:** If you have a rental car, keep it for this second week so that you can easily explore the area on day trips. Four-wheel drive is recommended but not required, unless you're making the trip to Punta Islita, as discussed below. See the Transportation Guide for this itinerary (p. 150) for more information.

The two major towns in the central Nicoya are Nosara and Sámara. Since they're just a short 30-45 minute drive apart, we recommend staying in one for the full week and visiting the other on day trips. Of the two, our pick for a laid-back beach vacation is Sámara.

Sámara is a quintessential beach town with restaurants, souvenir stands, boutique shops, and tour operators lining the main roads near the beach. Most of the businesses are located on the main strip or within walking distance on side roads. While Sámara does have plenty of restaurants and amenities, it still has a chill vibe and doesn't feel too developed. Lodging ranges from simple cabins and B&Bs to bungalows, luxury treehouses, and fully equipped vacation rentals. For dining, despite its small size, Sámara has lots of good choices. Casual and upscale eateries serve up Italian, French, contemporary American, authentic Costa Rican, fresh seafood, and even BBQ and healthy vegetarian/vegan options.

The Highlight

The highlight of Sámara is the main beach, Playa Sámara. Like many beaches in Guanacaste, Playa Sámara is very scenic, with light sand, a lush backing of tall palm trees, and turquoise water. But what makes this beach special is its combination of calm water and beachside dining. Playa Sámara is located in a cove so the ocean is much more tranquil and better for swimming than the surfing beaches to the north. And unlike some of the more remote swimming spots you will have visited earlier in your trip, Playa Sámara has a line of casual bars and restaurants just a stone's throw from the sea. Here, between dips in the ocean, you can grab a fruit smoothie or cocktail while still on the sand or shop the relaxed streets for souvenirs while you drip dry. Best of all, at sunset you can dine *al fresco* while watching the sun sink into the Pacific.

Beachside lounging at Playa Sámara

Day Trips to Other Nearby Beaches

Once you've spent some time at Playa Sámara, see what these other area beaches have to offer.

Playa Carrillo: Just a few kilometers to the south of Playa Sámara is the quiet Playa Carrillo. Grab some shade under the rows of coconut palms or have a picnic at the southern end. For a real taste of Tico culture, plan your visit for the weekend to see local families enjoying a typical beach day. Playa Carrillo doesn't have any amenities in the immediate vicinity so be sure to take whatever you need.

The Beaches of Nosara: About 30 km (19 miles) north of Sámara along a bumpy dirt road is another popular beach community, Nosara. Although in close proximity, Nosara has a completely different feel and is worth visiting for the day. Here, dirt roads run perpendicular to the beach, and residents get around the rough terrain mostly by ATV, motorcycle, or old 4x4. Although harder to access, the beaches of Nosara, Playa Guiones and Playa Pelada, are beautiful.

Playa Guiones, the longest and most popular of Nosara's beaches, is a 6 km (3.75 mile) stretch of white sand, which has big waves for surfing and fluffy sand dunes for sunbathing. A short walk away are surf shops, beach bars, and hotels. Playa Pelada, accessed by a different road to the north, is a smaller beach, which sits deep in a cove. This beach is striking with rocky points on both ends and is backed by palm and almond trees for shade. Although it may still have riptides, the beach is one of the better swimming beaches in Nosara. It also has a casual beach bar and restaurant called Olga's, which has been around for years and is a local favorite.

Activities and Attractions

When you're ready for a break from the sun, take in some of Costa Rica's amazing wildlife. **Sámara Trails** (p. 172), a 140 hectare (346 acre) private nature reserve within the Werner-Sauter Biological Reserve is a popular option for hiking. On a guided tour with a local expert, you'll learn about the flora and fauna of the tropical dry forest and have a chance to see howler monkeys, white-nosed coati, butterflies, and lots of birds.

For another nature-based day trip, head 45 minutes south to Punta Islita (four-wheel drive required). On a tour of the **Ara Project's** (p. 171) outdoor facility, you will learn about Scarlet and Great Green Macaw parrots and discover what efforts are being made to take them out of extinction. (Advanced reservations required.) If you're looking for a place to grab lunch in Punta Islita, this tiny village doesn't have many options, but there is a resort with a nice open-air restaurant overlooking the crescent-shaped beach.

On some of the beaches around Sámara, night turtle watching is also possible. Four types of sea turtles come to the shores south of town to lay their eggs, and sightings at Playa Camaronal are possible year-round. To the north, Playa Ostional near Nosara is known for its mass nesting events of olive ridley sea turtles, which occur with more regularity all year, but most often from August to December.

Finally, if you haven't had your fill of the ocean yet, get out on the bay for some water sports. Sámara's calmer seas offer small waves for beginner surfers as well as stand-up paddleboarding and kayaking. A popular excursion is a kayak-snorkel tour to the deserted **Isla Chora** (p. 171). Conditions for snorkeling vary seasonally so be sure to inquire before booking to ensure good visibility around the reef.

Other activities around Sámara include zip lining through the jungle, exploring the mountains on an ATV, horseback riding, dolphin-watching tours, and sportfishing.

10

COSTA RICA AND PANAMA

For the traveler who wants to see it all, the itinerary below will show you not one, but two countries in Central America. It may sound ambitious, but because of Costa Rica's small size, it is entirely possible to go from the capital city of San José to the tropical Caribbean coast and then south to Panama's Bocas del Toro islands in just one week. With two weeks, you can see the Caribbean coasts of Costa Rica and Panama plus some of Costa Rica's more diverse landscapes like cloud forests and even an active volcano.

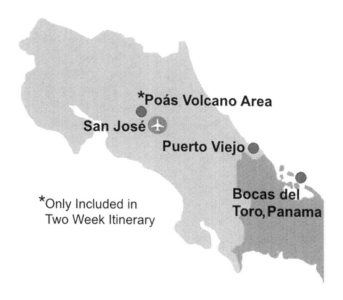

One Week Itinerary: Puerto Viejo de Talamanca, Costa Rica (4 days) to Bocas del Toro, Panama (3 days). Recommended Airport: SJO. View transportation options for this itinerary on p. 152.

Two Week Itinerary: Puerto Viejo de Talamanca, Costa Rica (6 days, includes day trip to Cahuita) to Bocas del Toro, Panama (5 days), to Poás Volcano (3 days). Recommended Airport: SJO. View transportation options for this itinerary on p. 153.

Puerto Viejo de Talamanca, Costa Rica

One Week Itinerary: Puerto Viejo de Talamanca, Costa Rica – Days 1-4

Two Week Itinerary: Puerto Viejo de Talamanca, Costa Rica – Days 1-6

Your Caribbean adventure begins in the laid-back town of Puerto Viejo de Talamanca on Costa Rica's southern Caribbean coast (about 4 hours from San José). The hub of this lively village is the busy but quaint downtown. Beside the palm-tree-lined, black sand beach, you'll find the majority of the area's eclectic restaurants and bars as well as souvenir stands, stores, and a few tour operators. Right offshore, you'll also notice the iconic Lanchón. This dock was involved in early attempts to extract oil from the region, but is no longer in use today and is now a popular hangout for local fishermen and kids.

Lodging in downtown Puerto Viejo consists mostly of budget options for the many backpackers, but there are plenty of mid- and high-end choices as well. Smaller communities to the south (Playa Cocles, Playa Chiquita, Playa Punta Uva, and Manzanillo) have lodging to suit any taste and budget, from modern vacation rentals to beachfront cottages and even treehouse lodges. Many travelers choose to rent a car to get around locally, but if you're staying close to the main road, you can easily get around by bicycle or taxi. Bike rentals are readily available, and at certain times of day, beach cruisers and rusty old ten-speeds far outnumber cars.

The Highlight

The highlight of Puerto Viejo is its vibrant culture. Unlike anywhere else in the country, the Caribbean coast has Afro-Caribbean roots that run deep. Many residents hail from the West Indies, originally coming to Costa Rica in the early days of the banana industry. They came for work and brought with them their unique heritage, which can be seen in everything from the bold food and upbeat music to the colorful homes and relaxed vibe. The laid-back island feel in Puerto Viejo is contagious, and after relaxing on the amazing beaches, tasting the fiery coconut curries, and kicking back to the Calypso beats, you'll definitely feel like you're on island time.

To delve deeper into the culture, take a tour through the local community tourism organization, **ATEC** (p. 170). On a visit to an indigenous community like the BriBri, you can learn more about another key group living on the Caribbean slope. A day tour or overnight stay will teach you about their traditional ways of life, customs, language, and methods of farming. You can visit a women's cooperative that grows organic bananas and other vegetables, all while using sustainable techniques and improving their standard of living, or take a cooking class where you'll learn to make (and get to taste) Caribbean cuisine.

Chilies are a common ingredient in local fare

Other Activities and Attractions

Once you've had your fill of culture, discover Costa Rica's diverse wildlife at the **Jaguar Rescue Center** (p. 171). This wildlife rehabilitation facility in Playa Chiquita is a favorite among travelers because it allows you to see rare rainforest animals close-up, like sloths, big cats, owls, and monkeys. On a guided tour, you'll hear stories of how the animals arrived at the center and also learn about the great work that the team of biologists and volunteers are doing every day to get these amazing creatures back into the wild.

Of course, any trip to the Caribbean wouldn't be complete without some towel time, and the beaches of Puerto Viejo are some of the best. Playa Cocles, just south of town, is a popular spot for surfing and people watching. This beach can get crowded, with sunbathers, surf instructors, and pop-up volleyball games, but still has plenty of space for everyone along the lengthy stretch of sand. Playa Punta Uva, 5 km (3 miles) farther south, is much more secluded and usually has calm waves, making it one of the best places in the area for swimming. The beach also features a coral ledge right offshore, which is good for casual snorkeling on calm days.

Other popular activities and attractions include visiting the **Ara Project** (p. 170) in Manzanillo to see rare Great Green Macaw parrots in the wild, hiking the rainforest at **Gandoca-Manzanillo National Wildlife Refuge** (p. 171), taking a chocolate tour, yoga classes, turtle watching (seasonal), and visiting the **Finca La Isla** botanical garden and farm (p. 171).

A Word of Caution: Always be aware of your surroundings in Puerto Viejo and never leave your belongings unattended. Puerto Viejo is generally safe but theft and crime are an occasional problem. It is best to be extra cautious by leaving your valuables locked in the safe of your hotel room. When going to the beach, take only your towel and sunscreen or make sure someone is watching your bag when you're swimming. Finally, a good practice no matter where you are in Costa Rica is to always lock your rental car and never leave anything in sight.

Cahuita, Costa Rica
(Day Trip from Puerto Viejo)

One Week Itinerary: Omitted. Go directly to Bocas del Toro.

Two Week Itinerary: Visit Cahuita on a day trip.

If you're on a two-week tour of Costa Rica and Panama, while in Puerto Viejo take a day trip to Cahuita just 20 minutes to the north. This peaceful village is home to **Cahuita National Park** (p. 156), which has nice walking trails that are good for all levels. The 8 km (5 mile) path follows the scenic coastline, but the real highlight is the howler monkeys, sloths, and bright yellow eyelash pit viper snakes, which can easily be spotted with some patience. After the park, head to one of the small restaurants in town to sample some local food or explore one of Cahuita's nearly deserted beaches like Playa Negra and Playa Grande.

Another popular day trip near Cahuita is the **Sloth Sanctuary** (p. 156). As the name implies, this facility is a sanctuary and rehabilitation center for sloths that have been injured or abandoned. Tours include a one-hour guided canoe ride and the chance to see some of the animals that the center cares for, including adorable baby sloths.

Bocas del Toro, Panama

One Week Itinerary: Bocas del Toro, Panama – Days 5-7

Two Week Itinerary: Bocas del Toro, Panama – Days 7-11

After you've experienced the culture of Costa Rica's Caribbean coast, see how Panama compares by heading south to the Bocas del Toro archipelago. Shuttles run daily from Puerto Viejo to the Bocas, making for an easy, short (four hours), and inexpensive trip.

The six islands of the Bocas are the epitome of tropical paradise, with clear water, beaches lined with swaying palm trees, and a laid-back atmosphere. Many of the hotels and restaurants are located right on the water, built on stilts or piers, so if you've always dreamed of waking up to the gentle swoosh of waves, the Bocas are for you.

When picking an island to stay on, keep in mind that each has a distinct feel. If you want to be close to all the amenities, consider Isla Colón. Colón is by far the busiest, most developed island and here you'll find many restaurants, bars, and shops. Colón is popular with backpackers and has a party scene, but if you stay out of the center of town, it is much quieter. If you're looking for something more peaceful and pristine, head to Isla Bastimentos, which offers luxurious eco-lodges set in the jungle, bungalows open to the sea, and also simple cabins and budget hostels near the town dock in Old Bank. Isla Carenero is a good middle ground, as it is much quieter than Isla Colón but just a two-minute boat ride away.

The Highlight

The highlight of the Bocas is island hopping. Once you step off the shuttle, you probably won't be in a car again until you're back on the mainland. The islands, with the exception of Isla Colón, don't have cars and the most common way to get around is by boat, bicycle, or on foot. Boat taxis are readily available and charge less than five dollars to get between many of the islands, making it fast and easy to explore. While cruising around the Bocas, you'll notice that each small skiff is as unique as the captain who is at the helm. Bright colors and eloquent names reflect the personalities of these fun-loving locals, all while giving each boat plenty of Caribbean flair.

Activities and Attractions

The main attraction in the Bocas is the beautiful beaches.

They're around every corner, but if you have time to see only one island, make it Isla Bastimentos. Here, you'll find Red Frog Beach and the more secluded Wizard Beach, two stunning golden sand beaches backed by thick jungle. They're known more for surfing so aren't the best for swimming but still worth the trip just for their raw beauty. While at Red Frog, be sure to ask a local to point out one of the tiny strawberry poison dart frogs that earned the beach its name.

Most people don't expect it from the more developed Isla Colón, but two unspoiled beaches lie just a half hour from the center of town. Boca del Drago and the adjacent Starfish Beach have some of the calmest water of the islands and are perfect for swimming and casual snorkeling. If you have a waterproof camera, it'll come in handy to photograph the giant red starfish. **Tip:** Avoid the temptation of picking up the starfish so that Starfish Beach doesn't lose these amazing creatures. *Inexpensive public shuttles leave from the center of town near the park about six times a day.*

One of the gigantic starfish visible through the crystal-clear water

For the best snorkeling around, take a boat tour to the distant **Cayos Zapatillas** (p. 155). Right from the shore, you can snorkel the shallow reef surrounding these uninhabited islands to see angel fish, grouper, snapper, parrot fish, and needlefish.

If you're looking for some adventure, we highly recommend the Nivida Bat Cave in Bahía Honda on Isla Bastimentos. This is an authentic tour where, with a local guide, you'll wade through a dark underground stream, exploring the cave's interesting rock formations and seeing hundreds of bats. Inquire with a local hotel on Bastimentos to find the best guide.

Other activities of interest are the Ngöbe indigenous community on Isla San Cristobal, the botanical garden at the **Monkey Farm** (p. 155), boat tours to Isla de Los Pájaros (Island of the Birds), diving, kayaking, dolphin watching, chocolate tours, and surfing on Islas Colón, Bastimentos, or Carenero.

Poás Volcano Area

One Week Itinerary: Omitted. Trip ends in Bocas del Toro.

Two Week Itinerary: Poás Volcano Area – Days 12-14

For the two-week traveler, after gallivanting around on Caribbean islands, return to Costa Rica's mainland to explore the mountains and famous Poás Volcano.

Poás Volcano isn't far from the Caribbean coast, but the landscape couldn't differ more. Located in the central volcanic mountain range, the Poás area has steep hills made lush and green by an abundance of rain and fog. Temperatures are on the cooler side (for the tropics) because of the higher elevation so be sure to pack some layers. Although many people visit Poás only on a day trip to see the volcano, it is worth spending a couple of nights in this serene, country setting. Pick a hotel that is close to the volcano so you can visit early in the morning before the cloud cover fills in. Lodging is available in the town of Vara Blanca, just a short drive to Poás, and in Poasito, closest to the park entrance.

Tip: Small plane flights from Isla Colón, Panama to San José, Costa Rica (near Poás) are a great way to avoid a long day of travel by land. Read more in our Transportation Guide (p. 153).

The Highlight

With the largest active crater in the world, Poás Volcano is undoubtedly the highlight of the area. Not only is the massive crater almost a mile (1.5 km) wide and 300 meters (900 feet) deep, but it features an almost out-of-this-world blue lake. You can view this impressive crater from above at the observation deck in **Poás Volcano National Park** (p. 169). The park has a few different well-maintained trails that go through the forest, but access to the main crater is along a nicely paved, wheelchair-accessible path.

Due to constantly shifting winds, the crater is often covered in clouds and not visible. Visit during the dry season of December to April for the best chances and arrive to the summit early as the clouds tend to thicken later in the day. This park is one of the most visited in Costa Rica so arriving early will also help you avoid the crowds.

Other Activities and Attractions

To learn more about Costa Rica's most famous crop, coffee, visit the **Doka Estate** (p. 169) just a short drive from Vara Blanca. On a tour, you'll get to see how Costa Rica's rich 100% Arabica java is made from bean to cup from one of the oldest producers in the country.

Another popular stop is the **La Paz Waterfall Gardens** (p. 169), a lodge and park with five waterfalls and nicely maintained animal enclosures. Spend the day exploring the hummingbird garden, butterfly garden, Serpentarium, frog exhibit, and jungle-cat enclosure, which houses rescued wild cats. You'll even have the chance to hold a toucan and feed a hummingbird.

For those up for a moderately difficult hike, there's **Catarata del Toro** (p. 169), a little-known waterfall in the town of Bajos del Toro. Believed to be one of Costa Rica's largest at 90 meters (300 feet), this waterfall, which flows into an extinct volcanic crater, won't remain a secret long. Catarata del Toro is on private property and accessed by hiking down around 375 rickety, steep steps.

While in the Poás area, also be sure to taste some of the local specialties. Palmito cheese, similar to fresh mozzarella, is made in the area, and don't miss the delicious strawberries, which you'll see growing along the hillside and find in everything from smoothies and jam to wine.

TRANSPORTATION GUIDE

Getting to Costa Rica

Costa Rica has two international airports. Juan Santamaría International (SJO) is located in the Central Valley near the capital city of San José and is the largest, busiest airport. Daniel Oduber Quirós International (LIR) is located in the city of Liberia in Guanacaste Province and is a newer, smaller airport, which is a good option for exploring the beaches of northwestern Costa Rica. Costa Rica also has two domestic airlines, Nature Air and Sansa, which provide service to and from the two main airports and smaller airstrips around the country as well as some destinations in the bordering countries of Panama and Nicaragua.

In addition to air travel, travelers may also enter Costa Rica by land. Two border crossings are located to the north along the Nicaragua border, Peñas Blancas and Los Chiles, and two are found to the south along the Panama border, Paso Canoas and Sixaola.

Getting Around in Costa Rica

Visitors to Costa Rica have many options for transportation. Rental cars, shuttle vans, domestic small planes, ferries, taxis, and both private and public buses reach almost every corner of the country. Rental cars are popular for those who want the freedom to stop and go as they please, and there are many agencies conveniently located throughout the country. Before renting a car, know that Costa Rica's roads are as diverse as its flora and fauna. Everything from flat, multi-lane highways with toll booths to rugged dirt roads with river crossings can be found. With a jagged topography and several impressive mountain ranges, the country's roadways also can be very steep and curvy. Be sure to determine if four-wheel drive is necessary to explore the areas you'll be visiting before selecting a rental.

Those wanting to leave the driving to someone else can easily do so. There are many shuttle companies that offer airport-to-hotel or hotel-to-hotel service in comfortable, air-conditioned vans. Private shuttles are available to take you anywhere in the country as well as shared shuttles (typically holding 8-19 passengers), which are more affordable and serve the major destinations. The two largest shared shuttle companies are Interbus and Grayline, though there are many others as well.

For shorter trips, taxis are a good option. Registered taxis are uniformly red or orange with a yellow medallion on the door. Always ask the driver to use the meter or otherwise negotiate a price before riding.

The fastest way to travel is to take a domestic flight on one of Costa Rica's two local carriers, Nature Air and Sansa, which serve many of Costa Rica's most popular destinations. These flights may be less expensive than you think and offer a bird's-eye view of the country.

For those wanting to save some money, the public bus is the most inexpensive option. While travel times are usually longer, the bus is fairly reliable and can take you just about anywhere in the country. For longer trips, opt for a direct bus (*directo*), which stops less often than collective buses (*colectivos*). It can be difficult to figure out the bus schedule in Costa Rica, but this website is a good place to start: http://www.thebusschedule.com/cr. Bus stations generally have up-to-date schedules posted and it is best to confirm times in advance with a ticket agent or knowledgeable local. Also be sure to buy tickets in advance for longer trips (e.g., to and from San José) as they sometimes sell out, especially on weekends.

What's Included in This Guide?

Below we provide information on the three primary modes of transportation that most travelers use: rental car, shared shuttle, and small plane flight. This information is intended to give you estimates of travel times and prices so that you can compare the options and choose what is best for you. Keep in mind that flight prices vary by season and availability. Shuttle prices remain fairly constant, but the length of trip can vary can depending on exact pickup and drop-off location as well as traffic.

For those choosing to drive, in addition to drive times, we provide general information on road conditions and explain when four-wheel drive is required. Cost for rentals will vary depending on the type of vehicle, company, season, and duration. But in general, the price for a mid-size SUV with four-wheel drive will be around $400-700 per week, and a four-door sedan will be around $300-500 per week. When comparing quotes, be sure that prices include Costa Rica's mandatory basic liability insurance.

If you have further questions or would like specific recommendations, feel free to ask us a question in the travel forum of our website. We often have special discounts for our readers on transportation like rental cars: http://www.twoweeksincostarica.com.

TRANSPORTATION OPTIONS
FOR EACH ITINERARY

BEST OF COSTA RICA

One Week Itinerary: Transportation

Each of the three main transportation options are available for this itinerary. See the details below for more information.

San José to La Fortuna

- Rental Car: 3-4 hrs. along mountainous paved roads.
- Shared Shuttle: 3.5-5 hrs. (around $50).
- Flight: 30 min. ($52-84).

La Fortuna to Manuel Antonio

- Rental Car: 4-5 hrs. along mountainous paved roads and flat highways.
- Shared Shuttle: 5-6 hrs. ($40-50).
- Flight: La Fortuna to Quepos 30 min. ($65-118).

Manuel Antonio to San José

- Rental Car: 2.5 hrs. along paved highway.
- Shared Shuttle: 4-4.5 hrs. (around $50).
- Flight: Quepos to San José 30 min. ($40-74).

Two Week Itinerary: Transportation

Each of the three main transportation options are available for different legs of this itinerary. For the trip from La Fortuna to Monteverde, if you rent a car, be sure to get four-wheel drive. If you would rather not drive, the Jeep-Boat-Jeep shuttle service from La Fortuna is a good alternative and breaks up the drive with a scenic boat ride. Several operators in La Fortuna offer this service.

For the trip from Manuel Antonio to Drake Bay, we recommend taking a shuttle or private transfer to Sierpe and then a boat transfer. At the end of your stay, you can then take a small plane back to San José from the airstrip in Drake. Alternatively, there are shuttles back to San José from Sierpe. Or if you drive, you can leave your rental car in a guarded lot in Sierpe, then retrieve it after your stay and drive back to San José yourself. Although it is possible to drive to Drake Bay, it is not recommended. The roads are rough dirt and there are multiple river crossings best forded by only the most experienced locals.

See the details below for more information.

San José to La Fortuna

- Rental Car: 3-4 hrs. along mountainous paved roads.
- Shared Shuttle: 3.5-5 hrs. (around $50).
- Flight: 30 min. ($52-84).

La Fortuna to Monteverde

- Rental Car: 3-4 hr. total trip. About 1.5 hrs. along windy lake road then rough dirt road after the town of Tilarán (about 2 hrs.). 4x4 required. Note: In the rainy season, road may have large ruts and occasional washouts.
- Shared Shuttle: 4-6 hrs., depending on company ($50).
- Jeep to Boat to Jeep (Best Option if Not Renting a Car): 3-4 hrs. ($25), includes pickup from hotel in La Fortuna,

30 min. boat ride across Lake Arenal, and drive to hotel in Monteverde.

- Flight: n/a

Monteverde to Manuel Antonio

- Rental Car: 3-4 hrs. along bumpy dirt road outside Monteverde then paved highway.
- Shared Shuttle: 4-6 hrs., depending on company ($50-60).
- Flight: n/a

Manuel Antonio to Drake Bay

- Rental Car: Driving to Drake Bay is not recommended. If you drive, leave your car in Sierpe (2 hrs. from Manuel Antonio) and then take a boat taxi to Drake Bay (about $20). Secure parking is available in Sierpe for around $6/day.
- Shuttle and Boat Taxi (Recommended): 2.5 hr. shuttle ride from Manuel Antonio to Sierpe ($45). Speedboat ride from the Las Vegas Restaurant to Drake (1 hr.), about $20. Ask your lodge in Drake Bay for help arranging the boat taxi.
- Flight: Flights available but not recommended due to layover in San José, which makes total travel time 3-5 hrs. ($85-163).

Drake Bay to San José

- Rental Car: From Sierpe to San José, around 4-5 hrs. along paved highway.
- Shared Shuttle: After taking a boat taxi from Drake, take a shuttle from Sierpe to San José, 4.5-7.5 hrs., depending on shuttle company ($65-95).
- Flight (Recommended): 45-60 min. ($85-136).

AUTHENTIC COSTA RICA

One Week Itinerary: Transportation

Because this itinerary includes towns that are not popular tourist destinations, shared shuttles and flights connect few of the destinations. Your best option is to rent a car or arrange private transfers. Alternatively, the public bus serves these destinations. Refer to this website for information on the bus schedule, http://www.thebusschedule.com/cr, and always confirm times with a ticket agent or local.

San José to Cahuita

- Rental Car: 3.5 hrs. along paved highway.
- Shared Shuttle: 4-5 hrs. (around $50).
- Flight: n/a

Cahuita to Grecia/Atenas

- Rental Car: 4-5 hrs. depending on traffic around San José. Conditions: highway and paved roads.
- Shared Shuttle: No shared shuttle direct to Grecia/Atenas. Could take shared shuttle to San José then private transportation (private shuttle, taxi) or the bus the rest of the way.
- Flight: n/a

Grecia/Atenas to San José

- Rental Car: 45 min. along paved roads and highway.
- Shared Shuttle: n/a
- Flight: n/a

Two Week Itinerary: Transportation

Because this itinerary includes towns that are not popular tourist destinations, shared shuttles and flights connect few of the destinations. Your best option is to rent a car or arrange private transfers. Alternatively, the public bus serves these destinations. Refer to this website for information on the bus schedule, http://www.thebusschedule.com/cr, and always confirm times with a ticket agent or local.

San José to Cahuita

- Rental Car: 3.5 hrs. along paved highway.
- Shared Shuttle: 4-5 hrs. (around $50).
- Flight: n/a

Cahuita to Turrialba

- Rental Car: 2.5 hrs. along paved highway.
- Shared Shuttle: n/a
- Flight: n/a

Turrialba to Grecia/Atenas

- Rental Car: Around 3 hrs. depending on traffic around San José. Conditions: paved roads and highway.
- Shared Shuttle: n/a
- Flight: n/a

Grecia/Atenas to Liberia/Guanacaste Province
(time est. based on Liberia)

- Rental Car: 3.5 hrs. along paved roads and highway.
- Shared Shuttle: n/a
- Flight: n/a

Liberia/Guanacaste Province
(time est. based on Liberia) to San José

- Rental Car: Around 4 hrs. depending on traffic. Conditions: paved highway.
- Shared Shuttle: 5 hrs. (around $50).
- Flight: 50-90 min., depending on airline ($59-106).

ADVENTURE

One Week Itinerary: Transportation

The main transportation options available for this itinerary are a rental car or shuttle. If you plan to do mostly adventure excursions through tour operators, you can easily take shuttles to get between destinations, as the tour companies will pick you up at your hotel. If you would rather have the flexibility explore on your own, however, you may want a car, especially for La Fortuna where things are more spread out.

San José to Jacó

- Rental Car: 1.5 hrs. along paved highway.
- Shared Shuttle: 2-2.5 hrs. (around $40).
- Flight: n/a

Jacó to La Fortuna

- Rental Car: Around 4 hrs. along highway and curvy paved roads.
- Shared Shuttle: 5-6 hrs. ($40-50).
- Flight: n/a

La Fortuna to San José

- Rental Car: Around 3 hrs. along mountainous paved roads.
- Shared Shuttle: 3-4 hrs. (around $50).
- Flight: 25-70 min., depending on airline ($52-84).

Two Week Itinerary: Transportation

Renting a car is the best option for this itinerary, but you could also take a combination of shared and private shuttles. If you rent a car, be sure to get four-wheel drive as the roads around Monteverde are rough dirt. If you plan to take shuttles, opt for the Jeep-Boat-Jeep service to get from Monteverde to La Fortuna, which includes a scenic boat ride across Lake Arenal. Several operators in La Fortuna offer this service.

San José to Jacó

- Rental Car: 1.5 hrs. along paved highway.
- Shared Shuttle: 2-2.5 hrs. (around $40).
- Flight: n/a

Jacó to Monteverde

- Rental Car: 3-4 hrs. along highway and mixture of paved roads and rough dirt roads outside Monteverde. 4x4 required.
- Shared Shuttle: 4-5 hrs. ($50).
- Flight: n/a

Monteverde to La Fortuna

- Rental Car: 3-4 hr. total trip along rough dirt roads (between Monteverde and Tilarán), then paved, windy lake road between Tilarán and La Fortuna. 4x4 required. Note: In the rainy season, roads around Monteverde may have large ruts and occasional washouts.
- Shared Shuttle: 4-6 hrs. depending on company ($40-50).
- Jeep to Boat to Jeep (Best Option if Not Renting a Car): 3-4 hrs. ($25), includes pickup from hotel in

Monteverde, 30 min. boat ride across Lake Arenal, and drive to hotel in La Fortuna.

- Flight: n/a

La Fortuna to Turrialba

- Rental Car: About 4 hrs. along paved roads and highway.
- Shared Shuttle: n/a
- Flight: n/a

Turrialba to San José

- Rental Car: 1.5-2 hrs. depending on traffic around San José. Conditions: Paved highway.
- Shared Shuttle: n/a
- Flight: n/a

SURFING

One Week Itinerary: Transportation

You won't need a rental car if you plan to surf only at the main beaches in Tamarindo and Playa Grande, but to explore some of the smaller beaches in the area, one is recommended. Opt for an SUV for carrying your board and check with the rental car company to see if they offer roof racks; some do.

Liberia to Tamarindo/Playa Grande

- Rental Car: 1 hr. along paved roads.
- Shared Shuttle: 1.5 hrs. ($40).
- Flight: Flight not recommended for this short trip.

Tamarindo/Playa Grande to Liberia

- Rental Car: 1 hr. along paved roads.
- Shared Shuttle: 1.5 hrs. (around $40).
- Flight: Flight not recommended for this short trip.

Two Week Itinerary: Transportation

Though you could get by without one, a rental car would give you the most flexibility to explore the smaller beaches included in this itinerary. An SUV is best for carrying your board; be sure it has four-wheel drive for the trip to Santa Teresa. For the final leg from Santa Teresa to Playa Hermosa (Jacó), you can either can drive around the Nicoya Peninsula or take a car ferry from Paquera to Puntarenas to save time. See below for more details.

Liberia to Tamarindo/Playa Grande

- Rental Car: 1 hr. along paved roads.
- Shared Shuttle: 1.5 hrs. ($40).
- Flight: Flight not recommended for this short trip.

Tamarindo/Playa Grande to Santa Teresa

- Rental Car: Around 4-5 hrs. Road is well paved until you get to S. Nicoya Peninsula (Naranjo), then it turns to a mixture of paved and dirt. The final 10 km (6 mile) stretch from Cóbano to Mal País is especially bumpy.
- Shared Shuttle: 4.5 hrs. ($50).
- Flight: Flights available (Tamarindo to Tambor) but not recommended due to layovers, which makes total trip 5-9 hrs. ($92-167).

Santa Teresa to Playa Hermosa (Jacó)

- Rental Car: Option 1: Drive from Santa Teresa to Playa Hermosa, 5-6 hrs. Option 2: Take car ferry from Paquera to Puntarenas ($1.50 per person, around $20 for the car), then drive south from Puntarenas to Playa Hermosa, 3.5 hrs. total (includes 1 hr. ferry ride).
- Speedboat Taxi from Montezuma to Playa Herradura: 1 hr. ($40). Herradura is about 20 min. north of Playa Hermosa.
- Flight: n/a

Playa Hermosa (Jacó) to Liberia

- Rental Car: 3-3.5 hrs. along paved highway.
- Shared Shuttle: Jacó to Liberia- 4 hrs. ($52).
- Flight: n/a

WILDLIFE

One Week Itinerary: Transportation

This itinerary includes Tortuguero, which is difficult to access and can be reached only by boat or plane. The easiest option for arranging transportation is to go through your hotel. Many hotels in Tortuguero include ground transportation to and from San José in their packages and can also help make arrangements for after you leave Tortuguero. If you would prefer to book everything yourself, it is possible. Small planes fly out of San José daily and are the fastest option. You can also take a shuttle, the public bus (least expensive), or drive and leave your car near the docks in La Pavona.

For getting from Tortuguero to Manuel Antonio, the fastest options are either to take a small plane or drive. You can also take the public bus right from the dock in La Pavona and get to Manuel Antonio via connection in San José. Lastly, you could take a shuttle to San José and a second shuttle from San José to Manuel Antonio.

See the details below for more information.

San José to Tortuguero

- Rental Car: 3-4 hrs. to dock in La Pavona (near Cariari), then 1-1.5 hr. boat ride to Tortuguero, $4. Be sure to get GPS to reach this remote area. Secure parking is available in La Pavona, $10/day.
- Shared Shuttle: 5-6 hrs. total, including boat ride to Tortuguero ($50-60).
- Flight: 30-60 min., depending on season ($59-107).

Tortuguero to Manuel Antonio

- Rental Car: Around 6 hrs. from La Pavona.
- Shared Shuttle: Tortuguero to San José, 5-6 hrs. (includes 1-1.5 hr. boat ride) ($50-60), then second shuttle from San José to Manuel Antonio, 3.5-4 hrs. ($50).
- Flight: Tortuguero to Quepos, 3 hrs., includes layover ($70-127).

Manuel Antonio to San José

- Rental Car: 2.5 hrs. along paved highway.
- Shared Shuttle: 4-5 hrs., depending on shuttle company (around $50).
- Flight: Quepos to San José 30 min. ($40-74).

Two Week Itinerary: Transportation

This itinerary includes Tortuguero and Drake Bay, which are difficult to access and can be reached only by boat or plane.

To get from Puerto Viejo to Tortuguero, the easiest option is to arrange transportation through your hotel. Many hotels in Tortuguero include transportation in their packages and can also help arrange transportation for after you leave Tortuguero. If you would prefer to make the arrangements yourself, you can also take a shuttle, the public bus (least expensive), or drive.

For getting from Tortuguero to Manuel Antonio, the fastest options are either to take a small plane or drive. You can also take the public bus right from the dock in La Pavona and get to Manuel Antonio via connection in San José. Lastly, you could take a shuttle to San José and a second shuttle from San José to Manuel Antonio.

For the trip from Manuel Antonio to Drake Bay, we recommend taking a shuttle or private transfer to Sierpe and then a boat transfer. At the end of your stay, you can then take a small plane back to San José from airstrip in Drake. Alternatively, there are shuttles back to San José from Sierpe, or if you drive, you can leave your rental car in a guarded lot in Sierpe, then retrieve it after your stay and drive back to San José yourself. Although it is possible to drive to Drake Bay, it is not recommended. The roads are rough dirt and there are multiple river crossings best forded by only the most experienced locals.

See the details below for more information.

San José to Puerto Viejo de Talamanca

- Rental Car: 4 hrs. along paved highway.
- Shared Shuttle: 4-5 hrs. ($50).
- Flight: n/a

Puerto Viejo de Talamanca to Tortuguero

- Rental Car: Option 1- Drive to boat docks in La Pavona (near Cariari), 3-4 hrs., then take a 1-1.5 hr. boat ride, $4. Option 2- Drive to Moín (near Limón), 1 hr., then take a longer 3-4 hr. boat ride, around $35-50/person (fare is negotiable depending on number of people, etc.). Secure parking is available in both La Pavona and Moín for a small fee.
- Shared Shuttle: Least expensive shuttle option is to take a shuttle to La Pavona, then a 1-1.5 hr. boat ride (5-6 hrs. total, $40-50). Other option is to take a shuttle to Moín near Limón, then a longer 3-4 hr. boat ride (5-6 hrs. total, $75).
- Flight: n/a

Tortuguero to Manuel Antonio

- Rental Car: Around 6 hrs. from either La Pavona or Moín.
- Shared Shuttle: Tortuguero to San José, 5-6 hrs. (includes 1-1.5 hr. boat ride) ($50-60), then second shuttle from San José to Manuel Antonio (3.5-4 hrs., $50).
- Flight: Tortuguero to Quepos, 3 hrs., includes layover ($70-127).

Manuel Antonio to Drake Bay

- Rental Car: Driving to Drake Bay is not recommended. If you drive, leave your car in Sierpe (2 hrs. from Manuel Antonio) and then take a boat taxi to Drake Bay (about $20). Secure parking is available in Sierpe for around $6/day.
- Shuttle and Boat Taxi (Recommended): 2.5 hr. shuttle ride from Manuel Antonio to Sierpe ($45). Speedboat ride from the Las Vegas Restaurant to Drake (1 hr.), about $20. Ask your lodge in Drake Bay for help arranging the boat taxi.
- Flight: Flights available but not recommended due to layover in San José, which makes total travel time 3-5 hrs. ($85-163).

Drake Bay to San José

- Rental Car: From Sierpe to San José, around 4-5 hrs. along paved highway.
- Shared Shuttle: After taking a boat taxi from Drake, take a shuttle from Sierpe to San José, 4.5-7.5 hrs., depending on shuttle company ($65-95).
- Flight (Recommended): 45-60 min. ($85-136).

BIRDING

One Week Itinerary: Transportation

Flights or shared shuttles are not available between these destinations so a rental car (four-wheel drive) or private shuttle is recommended for this itinerary.

Estimated Drive Times

- San José to Puerto Viejo de Sarapiquí: 1.5-2 hrs. along mountainous paved roads.
- Puerto Viejo de Sarapiquí to San Gerardo de Dota: 3.5-4 hrs. along mountainous paved roads. Avoid driving to San Gerardo de Dota at night. The road is narrow and windy, and visibility is often poor due to cloud cover.
- San Gerardo de Dota to San José: 2 hrs. along mountainous paved roads.

Two Week Itinerary: Transportation

Flights or shared shuttles are not available between these destinations so a rental car (four-wheel drive) or private shuttle is recommended for this itinerary.

Estimated Drive Times

- San José to Puerto Viejo de Sarapiquí: 1.5-2 hrs. along mountainous paved roads.
- Puerto Viejo de Sarapiquí to San Gerardo de Dota: 3.5-4 hrs. along mountainous paved roads. Avoid

driving to San Gerardo de Dota at night. The road is narrow and windy, and visibility is often poor due to cloud cover.

- San Gerardo de Dota to Costa Ballena: About 2 hrs. along mountainous paved roads.
- Costa Ballena to Tárcoles: 1.5-2 hrs. along flat paved roads.
- Tárcoles to San José: About 1 hr. along mountainous paved roads and highway.

FAMILY FUN

One Week Itinerary: Transportation

Flights are not recommended for this itinerary due to multiple layovers. Between a car and shuttle, a car may be the most economical choice given the cost for a family of 3 or more to take a shuttle. Having a car in La Fortuna and Nosara would also be convenient given that activities in these areas tend to be more spread out (four-wheel drive recommended for Nosara). If you prefer to take shuttles, be sure to weigh the cost of a shared versus private shuttle as it could be similar depending on the size of your family. Note that most shuttle companies charge a reduced rate (up to half price) for children.

Liberia to La Fortuna

- Rental Car: Around 3 hrs. along paved highway and curvy, paved lakeside road.
- Shared Shuttle: 4-5 hrs. ($39).
- Flight: Flights available but not recommended due to stops and layovers, which make travel time 4 plus hrs.

La Fortuna to Nosara

- Rental Car: 4-5 hrs. along paved roads and highway, then bumpy dirt roads outside Nosara.
- Shared Shuttle: n/a
- Flight: Flights available but not recommended due to stops and layovers, which make travel time 3 plus hrs. ($90-165).

Nosara to Liberia

- Rental Car: Around 2.5 hrs. along bumpy dirt roads outside Nosara and then paved roads.
- Shared Shuttle: 3.5 hrs. ($55).
- Flight: n/a

Two Week Itinerary: Transportation

Although there are other options, a rental car may be the most economical choice for this itinerary given the cost for 3 or more people to take a shuttle or small plane between destinations. Activities and attractions in La Fortuna and Nosara tend to be more spread out as well, so having a car also would be convenient (four-wheel drive recommended for Nosara). If you prefer to take shuttles, shared shuttles are available between some of the destinations and private shuttles for the remaining. Be sure to weigh the cost of a shared versus private shuttle as it could be similar depending on the size of your family. Note that most shuttle companies charge a reduced rate (up to half price) for children.

San José to La Fortuna

- Rental Car: 3-4 hrs. along mountainous paved roads.
- Shared Shuttle: 3.5-5 hrs. (around $50).
- Flight: 30 min. ($52-84).

La Fortuna to Nosara

- Rental Car: 4-5 hrs. along paved roads and highway then bumpy dirt roads outside Nosara.
- Shared Shuttle: n/a

- Flight: Flights available but not recommended due to stops and layovers, which make travel time 3 plus hrs. ($90-165).

Nosara to Manuel Antonio

- Rental Car: Around 5 hrs. along bumpy roads outside Nosara then paved roads and highway.
- Shared Shuttle: n/a
- Flight: Flights available (Nosara to Quepos) but not recommended due to layovers, which makes total trip 4-5 hrs. ($83-151).

Manuel Antonio to San José

- Rental Car: 2.5 hrs. along paved highway.
- Shared Shuttle: 4-5 hrs., depending on shuttle company (around $50).
- Flight: Quepos to San José, 30 min. ($40-74).

ECO-TREKKING

One Week Itinerary: Transportation

Though you could get between destinations by small plane or shuttle, you may want to rent a car for this itinerary. Having a car will give you more flexibility to explore the parks and reserves on your own, outside of organized excursions with tour operators. If you do rent a car, be sure to get four-wheel drive for the trip from La Fortuna to Monteverde. The Jeep-Boat-Jeep shuttle service from La Fortuna is a good alternative if you don't want to drive and includes a scenic boat ride. Several operators in La Fortuna offer this service.

Two Options for Arrival: SJO or LIR

Option 1: Liberia to La Fortuna

- Rental Car: Around 3 hrs. along paved highway and curvy, paved lakeside road.
- Shared Shuttle: 4-5 hrs. ($39).
- Flight: Flights available but not recommended due to stops and layovers, which make travel time 4 plus hrs.

Option 2: San José to La Fortuna

- Rental Car: 3-4 hrs. along mountainous paved roads.
- Shared Shuttle: 3.5-5 hrs. (around $50).
- Flight: 30 min. ($52-84).

Leg 2 of Trip: La Fortuna to Monteverde

- Rental Car: 3-4 hr. total trip. About 1.5 hrs. along

windy lake road then rough dirt road after the town of Tilarán (about 2 hrs.). 4x4 required. Note: In rainy season, road may have large ruts and occasional washouts.

- Shared Shuttle: 4-6 hrs., depending on shuttle company ($50).
- Jeep to Boat to Jeep (Best Option if Not Renting a Car): 3-4 hrs. ($25), includes pickup from hotel in La Fortuna, 30 min. boat ride across Lake Arenal, and drive to hotel in Monteverde.
- Flight: n/a

Two Options for Departure: SJO or LIR

Option 1: Monteverde to Liberia

- Rental Car: 2.5-3 hrs. along bumpy dirt roads outside Monteverde then paved highway.
- Shared Shuttle: 3.5 hrs. (around $50).
- Flight: n/a

Option 2: Monteverde to San José

- Rental Car: Around 3.5 hrs. along bumpy dirt roads outside Monteverde then paved highway.
- Shared Shuttle: 4-5 hrs. (around $50).
- Flight: n/a

Two Week Itinerary: Transportation

A rental car is recommended for this itinerary so that you have the flexibility to explore the parks and reserves on your own. Some of the destinations, notably the Southern Zone, are also more spread out so having a car would be convenient. If you rent a car, be sure to get four-wheel drive for trip from La Fortuna to Monteverde.

For the trip from the Southern Zone to Drake Bay, we recommend returning the rental car and taking a shuttle or private transfer to Sierpe and then a boat transfer. At the end of your stay, you can then take a small plane back to San José from the airstrip in Drake. Alternatively, there are shuttles back to San José from Sierpe, or if you drive, you can leave your rental car in a guarded lot in Sierpe, then retrieve it after your stay and drive back to San José yourself. Although it is possible to drive to Drake Bay, it is not recommended. The roads are rough dirt and there are multiple river crossings best forded by only the most experienced locals.

See the details below for more information.

San José to La Fortuna

- Rental Car: 3-4 hrs. along mountainous paved roads.
- Shared Shuttle: 3.5-5 hrs. (around $50).
- Flight: 30 min. ($52-84).

La Fortuna to Monteverde

- Rental Car: 3-4 hr. total trip. About 1.5 hrs. along windy lake road then rough dirt road after the town of Tilarán (about 2 hrs.). 4x4 required. Note: In rainy season, road may have large ruts and occasional washouts.
- Shared Shuttle: 4-6 hrs., depending on shuttle company ($50).
- Jeep to Boat to Jeep (Best Option if Not Renting a Car): 3-4 hrs. ($25), includes pickup from hotel in La Fortuna, 30 min. boat ride across Lake Arenal, and drive to hotel in Monteverde.
- Flight: n/a

Monteverde to Southern Zone
(Dominical/Uvita)

- Rental Car: 4-4.5 hrs. along bumpy roads outside Monteverde then smooth highway.
- Shared Shuttle: 6-7 hrs. ($70-80).
- Flight: n/a

Southern Zone (Dominical/Uvita)
to Drake Bay

- Rental Car: Driving to Drake Bay is not recommended. If you drive, leave your car in Sierpe (1 hr. south of Dominical) and then take a boat taxi to Drake Bay (about $20). Secure parking is available in Sierpe for around $6/day.
- Shuttle and Boat Taxi (Recommended): 1.5 hr. shuttle ride from Dominical or Uvita to Sierpe ($35). Speedboat ride from the Las Vegas Restaurant to Drake (1 hr.), about $20. Ask your lodge in Drake Bay for help arranging the boat taxi.
- Flight: n/a

Drake Bay to San José

- Rental Car: From Sierpe to San José, around 4-5 hrs. along paved highway.
- Shared Shuttle: After taking a boat taxi from Drake, take a shuttle from Sierpe to San José, 4.5-7.5 hrs., depending on shuttle company ($65-95).
- Flight (Recommended): 45-60 min. ($85-136).

GUANACASTE BEACHES

One Week Itinerary: Transportation

A rental car is recommended for this itinerary so that you have flexibility to explore the smaller beaches to the north and south of Tamarindo and Flamingo. Rental cars are available at the airport in Liberia. Although most of the roads in this area are well paved, some of the more remote beaches like Playa Avellanas and Playa Negra are located along bumpy dirt roads so a vehicle with higher ground clearance would be more comfortable.

Liberia to Tamarindo/Flamingo

- Rental Car: 1 hr. along paved roads.
- Shared Shuttle: 1.5 hrs. ($40).
- Flight: Flight not recommended for this short trip.

Tamarindo/Flamingo to Liberia

- Rental Car: 1 hr. along paved roads.
- Shared Shuttle: 1.5 hrs. ($40).
- Flight: Flight not recommended for this short trip.

Two Week Itinerary: Transportation

A rental car is recommended for this itinerary so that you have flexibility to explore the smaller beaches around Tamarindo/Flamingo and Sámara. Rental cars are available at the airport in Liberia. Although most of the roads in these areas are well paved, some of the beaches (Playa

Avellanas, Playa Negra, and those in Nosara) are located along bumpy dirt roads so a vehicle with higher ground clearance would be more comfortable. Note: If you plan to make the day trip to Punta Islita from Sámara, four-wheel drive is required.

Liberia to Tamarindo/Flamingo

- Rental Car: 1 hr. along paved roads.
- Shared Shuttle: 1.5 hrs. ($40).
- Flight: Flight not recommended for this short trip.

Tamarindo/Flamingo to Sámara

- Rental Car: Around 2 hrs. along paved roads.
- Shared Shuttle: 3 hrs. ($45-60).
- Flight: n/a

Sámara to Liberia

- Rental Car: 2 hrs. along paved roads.
- Shared Shuttle: 2-3 hrs. ($40-50).
- Flight: n/a

COSTA RICA AND PANAMA

One Week Itinerary: Transportation

Since you'll be traveling to more than one country in this itinerary, special considerations apply. To get from San José to Puerto Viejo, we recommend taking a shuttle or renting a car in San José and returning it in Puerto Viejo before heading to Bocas del Toro (Note: Only a couple of rental car companies are located in Puerto Viejo, Adobe and Alamo). To get to the Bocas, you'll take a shuttle, then a short boat taxi to reach the islands. On the return, you can take a shuttle back to San José or save a day of travel by taking a small plane. Be sure to inquire with the shuttle company about visa requirements for entry into Panama.

San José to Puerto Viejo de Talamanca

- Rental Car: 4 hrs. along paved highway.
- Shared Shuttle: 4-5 hrs. ($50).
- Flight: n/a

Puerto Viejo de Talamanca to Bocas del Toro, Panama

- Rental Car: n/a
- Shared Shuttle (Caribe Shuttle): 4 hrs. ($32), includes transportation from hotel in Puerto Viejo to dock in Bocas Town, Isla Colón, Panama.
- Flight: n/a

Bocas del Toro, Panama to San José

- Rental Car: n/a

- Shared Shuttle (Caribe Shuttle): 10 hrs. ($75), includes pickup from dock in Bocas Town, Isla Colón, Panama, lunch, and transportation to San José airport and hotels.
- Flight (Nature Air): 1 hr., $104-188.

Two Week Itinerary: Transportation

As with the one-week itinerary, special considerations apply to this itinerary since you'll be traveling to more than one country. To get from San José to Puerto Viejo, we recommend taking a shuttle or renting a car in San José and returning it in Puerto Viejo before heading to Bocas del Toro (Note: Only a couple of rental car companies are located in Puerto Viejo, Adobe and Alamo). To get to the Bocas, you'll take a shuttle, then a short boat taxi to reach the islands. Be sure to inquire with the shuttle company about visa requirements for entry into Panama. On the return, you can take a shuttle back to San José or save a day of travel by taking a small plane. To get from San José to the Poás area, you can then rent a car or arrange a private transfer for the 45-minute trip.

San José to Puerto Viejo de Talamanca

- Rental Car: 4 hrs. along paved highway.
- Shared Shuttle: 4-5 hrs. ($50).
- Flight: n/a

Puerto Viejo de Talamanca to
Bocas del Toro, Panama

- Rental Car: n/a
- Shared Shuttle (Caribe Shuttle): 4 hrs. ($32), includes

transportation from hotel in Puerto Viejo to dock in Bocas Town, Isla Colón, Panama.

- Flight: n/a

Bocas del Toro, Panama to Poás Volcano

- Rental Car: n/a
- Shared Shuttle (Caribe Shuttle): Shuttle from Bocas del Toro to San José (10 hrs., $75, includes pickup from dock in Bocas Town, Isla Colón, Panama and lunch). Then take a private transfer from San José to Poás Volcano area.
- Flight (Recommended): Bocas del Toro to San José, 1 hr., $104-188 (Nature Air). Then take a private transfer from San José to Poás Volcano area.

Poás Volcano to San José

- Rental Car: Around 45 min. along paved mountainous roads.
- Shared Shuttle: n/a
- Flight: n/a

ACTIVITIES GUIDE

Below is additional information on many of the attractions and activities included in this book. Where available, business hours, website, phone number, and tour information (duration and price) is provided. This guide is organized by town, alphabetically.

Bocas del Toro, Panama

Cayos Zapatillas: Snorkel tours are available through many operators in the Bocas. Prices are around $35 (includes park fee) and last about 6 hrs. Most operators stop at Coral Cay for lunch where there is a restaurant (cash only). Cayos Zapatillas has some trails too so bring proper footwear if you plan to explore.

Monkey Farm (Isla Colón): Guided Garden Tour (2 hrs.) $15, Mon. 1:00 p.m. and Fri. 8:30 a.m., other times by appointment. Guided Birding Tour $35 (4 person min.; reservations required), 6:30 a.m. and 4:30 p.m. http://www.bocasdeltorobotanicalgarden.com. (507) 757-9461 or 6729-9943.

Cahuita

ATEC (Talamancan Association of Ecotourism and Conservation) (Puerto Viejo): Reservations required for all tours, pickup available in Cahuita. Kèköldi indigenous territory (BriBri) tour (3.5 hrs.) $36. El Yüe Agroeco women's cooperative medicinal plants and farm tour (3 hrs.) $25, overnight with meals and lodging $65. Yorkin (BriBri) women's artisan group full-day cultural tour, $88. Overnight with meals and lodging, $108. Caribbean cooking class (2-3 hrs.) $55-65, 2 person min. http://www.ateccr.org. (506) 2750-0398.

Cacao Trails (Hone Creek): Chocolate Tour (45 min.) $15. Open daily 8:00 a.m.–3:00 p.m. Reservations encouraged. http://www.cacaotrails.com. (506) 2756-8186.

Cahuita National Park: Admission $5. Playa Blanca sector open daily 6:00 a.m.–5:00 p.m. Puerto Vargas sector open daily 8:00 a.m.–4:00 p.m. (closed 1st Mon. each month).

Sloth Sanctuary: Buttercup Tour (2 hrs.) $25, Tues.–Sun., 8:00 a.m.–2:00 p.m. starting on the hour. Insider Tour (4 hrs.) $150, Tues.–Sun., 7:45 a.m. and 10:45 a.m. (reservations required). http://www.slothsanctuary.com. (506) 2750-0775.

Tree of Life Wildlife Rescue Center & Botanical Gardens: Self-guided visits $12. Guided private tours $20 (4 person min., reservations required). Open Nov. 1 to Apr. 14, Tues.–Sun., 9:00 a.m.–3:00 p.m. Closed Apr. 15 to Jun. 30. Open Jul. 1 to Aug. 31, Tues.–Sun., one daily guided tour only at 11:00 a.m. Closed Sept. 1 to Oct. 31. http://www.treeoflifecostarica.com. (506) 8610-0490.

Central Valley (including Grecia and Atenas)

El Toledo Coffee (Atenas): Guided tour (2 hrs.) $15. Schedule varies by season, generally Sun.–Thurs. Reservations required. http://eltoledocoffee.weebly.com.

Espíritu Santo Coffee (Naranjo): Guided tour (1.5 hrs.) $22. Daily at 8:00 a.m., 9:00 a.m., 10:00 a.m., 11:00 a.m., 1:30 a.m., and 3:00 p.m. Reservations recommended. http://www.espiritusantocoffeetour.com. (506) 2450-3838.

Gold Museum (San José): Admission $10.50. Open daily 9:15 a.m.–5:00 p.m. (4:30 p.m. last entrance). Guided tours also available (1 hr.) $60 plus admission fee, reservations required at least 48 hrs. in advance. http://www.museosdelbancocentral.org/eng. (506) 2243-4202.

Jade Museum (San José): Admission $15. Open daily 10:00 a.m.–5:00 p.m. http://portal.ins-cr.com/portal.ins-cr.com/Social/MuseoJ/. (506) 2287-6034.

Los Chorros Waterfalls (Grecia): Directions: Go south on the main road out of town, Route 118, for about 8 km (5 miles). Shortly after the university, you'll approach a few businesses/small grocery stores in the small town of Tacares. Take a left after a small church onto Route 722 (unmarked). Immediately, you'll come to a fork. Take a left at the fork onto the road that goes uphill. Drive about 5 min. past sugarcane fields. Parking lot is in a field at the top of hill on the right just before the road curves sharply to the left. $4/vehicle to park. Entrance to waterfall trail is at the bottom of the hill, $6/person.

National Artisans Market (San José): Located across from the National Museum. No set hours.

National Museum (San José): Admission $8. Tues.–Sat., 8:30 a.m.–4:30 p.m. Sun. 9:00 a.m.–4:30 p.m. http://www.museocostarica.go.cr/. (506) 257-1433.

National Theater (San José): Guided tours $7, daily 9:00 a.m.–3:00 p.m. on the hour. https://www.teatronacional.go.cr. (506) 2010-1131 or 2010-1110.

Costa Ballena/Southern Zone (Dominical and Uvita)

Chirripó National Park (San Gerardo de Rivas): Admission $18 (must be paid in advance). Open daily 5:00 a.m.–10:00 a.m. (506) 2742-5083.

Cloudbridge Nature Reserve (San Gerardo de Rivas): Self-guided hiking trails. Donation only. http://www.cloudbridge.org.

Hacienda Barú Wildlife Refuge (Dominical): Self-guided hike $7. Guided tours starting at $25, reservations required. Open daily sunrise to sunset. http://www.haciendabaru.com. (506) 2787-0003.

Marino Ballena National Park (Uvita): Admission $12. Open daily 7:00 a.m.–4:00 p.m. Note: Admission ticket grants access to all four park entrances.

Nauyaca Waterfalls (near Platanillo): Horseback tour (6 hrs.) $70. Mon.–Sat. at 8:00 a.m., reservations required. Self-guided hike $5 through Don Lulo office, open daily, 8:00 a.m.–4:00 p.m. http://cataratasnauyaca.com. (506) 2787-0541.

Oro Verde Nature Reserve (Uvita): Guided birding tour (3 hrs.) $35. Daily 6:00 a.m. or 4:00 p.m. Reservations required through the Uvita Information Center: http://www.uvita.info/uvita/oro-verde-nature-reserve; (506) 2743–8889 or 8843-7142.

Piedras Blancas National Park/Esquinas Rainforest Lodge (La Gamba): Self-guided hike $5. Open daily at 7:00 a.m. Guided nature hike (3 hrs.) $15 (4 person min., $30 if less). Guided Birding Tour (1.5 hrs.) $15 (4 person min., $30 if less). Reservations required for guided tours.

Rubber boots and bug nets available for rent. http://www.esquinaslodge.com. (506) 2741-8001.

Rancho La Merced (Uvita): Self-guided hike $6. Guided hike $35 and guided birding tour $45, reservations required. Open daily 7:30 a.m.–5:30 p.m. http://www.rancholamerced.com/en. (506) 2743-8032 or (506) 8861-5147.

Tesoro Escondido Reserve: Guided hiking tours (4 hrs.) $29. Guided birding tour (4 hrs.) $34. Reservations required through Playa HermOSA Ecological Association: http://www.ecoreservaplayahermosa.com; (506) 8742-7877 for English/German or (506) 8839-8223 and (506) 8881-4996.

Whale Watching: Several operators in Dominical and Uvita offer whale and dolphin watching tours. Prices range from $70-85 for 3-4 hrs., includes snorkel equipment, water, and fruit.

Drake Bay

Caño Island: Several operators in Drake Bay offer snorkel and dive tours. Snorkel tour (6 hrs.) $80, includes transportation, lunch, and guide. Dive tour (6-7 hrs.) $135 for 2 dives, includes equipment, transportation, lunch, and guide.

Corcovado National Park (Osa Peninsula): Admission $15. Open daily, 7:00 a.m.–4:00 p.m. Sirena sector closed for the month of October for maintenance and because of heavy rainfall. All visits must be arranged through a registered guide. Day trips to Sirena Ranger Station or San Pedrillo Ranger Station, $80-90 for half day, includes boat transportation, lunch, and guided hike. Overnight visits to

Sirena Ranger Station, $250-300, includes boat transportation, meals, lodging at ranger station, and guided hikes. Longer visits can also be arranged; contact a tour operator in Drake Bay for rates.

Night Walk: Several operators in Drake Bay offer tours. Prices range from $35-50 (2-2.5 hrs.). Be sure to make reservations in advance as tour group sizes are limited.

Guanacaste/Liberia Area

Guaitil Pottery: Visitors can go to the village of Guaitil on their own and visit the shops, or arrange an organized tour. Tours typically combine a visit to Guaitil with a boat tour of Palo Verde National Park, $75-100.

Horseback Riding: There are many operators to choose from in the beach towns of Tamarindo, Flamingo, Brasilito, and Playa Hermosa. Tours are also popular near Rincon de la Vieja National Park, where they are sometimes combined with zip lining, hot springs, and other activities. Prices range from $25-100, depending on type and length of tour.

Las Pumas Rescue Center (Cañas): Self-guided walk $10. Mon.–Sun., 8:00 a.m.–4:00 p.m. http://www.centrorescatelaspumas.org/en. (506) 2669-6019.

Llanos de Cortéz Waterfall (Bagaces): Entrance fee by donation; money goes to local school. $2 vehicle charge at parking area (separate from donation).

Rincon de la Vieja National Park: Admission $15. Santa María sector open daily, 8:00 a.m.–4:00 p.m., Las Pailas sector open Tues.–Sun., 7:00 a.m.–3:00 p.m. Trail to the summit of the volcano closed at the time of this writing due to activity.

Santa Rosa National Park: Admission $15. Open daily, 8:00 a.m.–4:00 p.m.

Jacó and Tárcoles

All-in-One Adventure Tour: Jacó has many tour operators that offer combination adventure tours. Packages typically include transportation, guides, and a meal or snack. Prices range from $75-165 depending on what is included.

Carara National Park (Tárcoles): Admission $10. Open daily, 8:00 a.m.–4:00 p.m. (May to November) and 7:00 a.m.–3:00 p.m. (December to April). Ticket booth is closed for lunch from 12:00 p.m.–12:45 p.m. daily.

Crocodile Tour (Tárcoles): Several companies offer crocodile tours up the Tárcoles River. Prices are $30-50 for a 2 hr. tour. Reservations recommended.

Mountain Biking: Mountain biking tours are available through several operators in Jacó. Prices are around $60. Bike rentals are around $20/day. For local trail maps, including difficulty level, visit http://www.wikiloc.com/trails/outdoor/costa-rica/puntarenas/jaco.

Tortuga Island: Several operators in the Jacó area offer snorkel and dive tours. Snorkel tour: prices range from $100-145 for a full day, includes transportation, lunch, kayaking, and beach equipment. Diving tour: prices are around $130 (4-5 hrs.), includes transportation, refresher course (if needed), 2 dives, and a snack.

La Fortuna/Arenal Volcano Area

Arenal 1968 Trails: Self-guided hike $10. Open daily 8:00 a.m.–7:00 p.m. (506) 2462-1212.

Arenal Oasis Wildlife Refuge: Guided night tours begin at 5:45 p.m. (2-2.5 hrs.) $40. Reservations required. http://www.arenaloasis.com. (506) 2479-9526.

Arenal Observatory: Self-guided hike $8. Guided hikes also available. Open 7:00 a.m.–4:00 p.m. http://www.arenalobservatorylodge.com. (506) 2479-1070.

Arenal Volcano National Park: Admission $15. Open daily, 8:00 a.m.–4:00 p.m.

Baldi Resort: Hot springs day pass $31 adult, $15.50 children under six. Open daily 10:00 a.m.–10:00 p.m. https://www.baldihotsprings.cr. (506) 2479-2190.

Canyoning: A few operators in La Fortuna offer tours. Prices are typically $100 for a 3.5-4 hr. tour and include transportation and lunch.

Cerro Chato Hike: Access through Arenal Observatory (see above) or Green Lagoon Falls Park and Lodge, self-guided hike $10. Opens at 7:00 a.m. http://www.greenlagoon.net. (506) 2479-7700 or (506) 2479-7701.

EcoCentro Danaus: Guided night tours begin at 5:45 p.m. (2 hrs.) $37. Reservations required. http://www.ecocentrodanaus.com/en. (506) 2479-7019 or (506) 8928-1478.

Hot Springs: Many hotels and resorts in the La Fortuna area have on-site hot springs and allow public access for a fee. There are also a few standalone hot springs resorts. Day passes for the most popular resorts cost $30-70 (more for packages that include meals). The resorts vary in size and feel; some are naturally landscaped while others are more manmade, and some offer other features such as waterslides and swim-up bars. Be sure to book in advance as some of the resorts limit the number of visitors per day.

La Fortuna Waterfall: Access through Visitor Center $10. Open daily 8:00 a.m.–5:00 p.m. http:// www.arenaladifort.com. (506) 2479-9515. Several operators also offer a combination horseback tour and hike to the waterfall (4 hrs.), $60-80.

Mistico Arenal Hanging Bridges Park (formerly Arenal Hanging Bridges): Self-guided walk $24. Open daily 7:30 a.m.–4:00 p.m. Birding and natural history guided tours available with advanced reservations. http://misticopark.com. (506) 2479-1128.

Proyecto Asis (Ciudad Quesada): Guided wildlife center tour (1.5 hrs.), daily 8:30 a.m. and 1:00 p.m., $29 adults, $17 children (ages 4-9). Volunteering tour (3.5 hrs.), same hours, $51 adults, $29 children (ages 4-9). Reservations required at least one day in advance for all tours. http://www.institutoasis.com. (506) 2475-9121 or (506) 8722-8282.

Rainforest Chocolate Tour: Tours daily 8:00 a.m., 10:00 a.m., 1:00 p.m., and 3:00 p.m. (1.5 hrs.) $22. Reservations required. http:// www.rainforestchocolatetour.com. (506) 8474-4007.

Tenorio Volcano National Park (Bijagua): Self-guided walk $12. Open daily 8:00 a.m.–4:00 p.m. Last entrance into the park is at 2:00 p.m. Several operators also offer tours from La Fortuna, $80-120 for full day, includes transportation, lunch, and guided tour.

Venado Caves (Venado): Guided tour $22. Open daily 8:00 a.m.–3:00 p.m. http://www.cavernasdelvenadocr.com. (506) 2478-8008. Several operators in La Fortuna also offer transportation and tour packages to the caves.

White-Water Rafting: Several operators in the La Fortuna area offer tours. Prices range from $70-130 depending on the river and level of difficulty. The duration also varies from 4.5 hrs. for the closer Balsa River to 7 hrs. for rivers like the Sarapiquí, which are farther away. Tours include transportation and lunch.

Windsurfing/Kitesurfing: Rentals at Tico Wind start around $90, includes lunch. Windsurfing lessons (1 hr.) $50. Kitesurfing lessons (3 hrs.) $220. E-mail: info@ticowind.com. (506) 2692-2002 or (506) 8383-2694. http://www.ticowind.com/.

Manuel Antonio/Quepos Area

Catamaran Tour: Several operators in Manuel Antonio and Quepos offer morning and sunset tours. Around $75 (4-5 hrs.), includes transportation, snorkel equipment, drinks, snacks, and one meal. Discounts may be available for children under 6.

Isla Damas Mangrove Tour: Kayaking and boat tours available through many operators in Manuel Antonio and Quepos. Prices range from $60-70 for a half day, includes transportation and lunch.

Kids Saving the Rainforest/Sloth Institute (Quepos): Wildlife Sanctuary Tour, 9:00 a.m. Mon., Wed., Fri., and

Sun. (2 hrs.), reservations required. Suggested minimum donation of $40 for adults and $25 for children under 18. http://kidssavingtherainforest.org. (506) 2777-2572 or (506) 2777-1548 or (506) 2777-2592.

Manuel Antonio National Park: Admission $16. Open daily, 7:00 a.m.–4:00 p.m., except Jul. 1–Nov. 30 when the park is closed on Mondays.

Playa Biesanz Directions: At the top of the hill in Manuel Antonio, take a right after Barba Roja restaurant toward Punto Quepos/La Mariposa Hotel. Follow the road almost to the end. The entrance to the trail to the beach is an opening in a fence at the very bottom of the hill about 100 meters from the Parador Resort. Look for two small concrete posts on the right. People typically park along the side of the road. During the high season, someone may be there to watch cars in exchange for a tip. To reach the beach, walk about 5 minutes through the woods.

Rainforest Spices (outside of Quepos): Guided spice farm tour, around $45 (2-2.5 hrs.), includes transportation and a tasting. Tours Mon.–Sat. 9:00 a.m. and 1:00 p.m. Sunday only at 9:00 a.m. Reservations required. http://www.rainforestspices.com. (506) 8839-2721 or (506) 2779-1155.

Rainmaker Park (Parrita): Self-guided hike $15. Open daily 7:00 a.m.–6:00 p.m. Guided tours (river walk and canopy, birding, and night walk) available with reservation. http://www.rainmakercostarica.org. (506) 2777-3565 or (506) 8960-3836.

Zip-line Tour: Several companies in Quepos and Manuel Antonio offer tours. Prices for a standard canopy tour range from $65-75, 3-5 hrs. (some companies are farther away so travel time is longer), includes transportation and breakfast or lunch.

Monteverde and Santa Elena

ATV Tour: A few operators in the Monteverde area offer tours. Prices for a standard 3 hr. tour are around $50-60.

Bat Jungle: Guided tour (45 min.) $12. Open daily 9:00 a.m.–7:00 p.m. (9:30 a.m. Sun.). Best to arrive around the start of the hour for the tour. http://batjungle.com. (506) 2645-7701.

Children's Eternal Rainforest: Self-guided hike from Bajo del Tigre entrance $12. Open daily 7:30 a.m.– 5:30 p.m. Guided hike $28, daily 8:00 a.m. and 2:00 p.m., reservations required. http://acmcr.org. (506) 2645-5305.

Curi Cancha Reserve: Self-guided hike $14. Open daily 7:00 a.m.–3:00 p.m. Guided tours daily 7:30 a.m., 11:30 a.m., and 1:30 p.m. (3 hrs.) $29, reservations required. http://www.curi-cancha.com. (506) 2645-6915 or (506) 8356-1431.

Don Juan Coffee: Guided combination coffee-sugarcane-chocolate tour (2 hrs.) $30. Daily at 8:00 a.m., 10:00 a.m., 1:00 p.m., and 3:00 p.m. Reservations required. https://www.donjuancoffeetour.com. (506) 2645-7100 or (506) 2645-6858.

El Cafetal Coffee: Guided coffee-plantation tour (2 hrs.) $35. Daily at 8:00 a.m. and 2:00 p.m. Reservations required. http://yavagu.com. (506) 2645-7329 or (506) 8302-2769.

El Trapiche Coffee: Guided combination coffee-sugarcane-chocolate tour (2 hrs.) $32. Daily at 10:00 a.m. and 3:00 p.m. (Sun. 3:00 p.m. only). Reservations required. http://www.eltrapichetour.com. (506) 2645-7780 or (506) 2645-7650.

Hummingbird Gallery: Outside the entrance to Monteverde Cloud Forest Reserve. $2 donation to enter or purchase of item in gift shop. Open daily 8:00 a.m.–5:00 p.m. (506) 2645-5030.

Monteverde Cheese Factory: Facility tour, slideshow, and tasting $12. Mon.–Sat. 9:00 a.m. and 2:00 p.m. Morning tour recommended. http://monteverdecheesefactory.com. (506) 2645-7090.

Monteverde Cloud Forest Reserve: Self-guided hike $18. Open daily 7:00 a.m.–4:00 p.m. Guided natural history walk (2.5 hrs.) $36, daily at 7:30 a.m., 11:30 a.m., and 1:30 p.m. Guided night walk (2 hrs.) $17, daily at 5:45 p.m. Reservations recommended for guided activities. http://www.reservamonteverde.com. (506) 2645-5122.

Santa Elena Cloud Forest Reserve: Self-guided hike $14. Open daily 7:00 a.m.–4:00 p.m. Guided hike $29 (2.5-3 hrs.), 7:30 a.m., 9:00 a.m., 11:30 a.m., and 1:00 p.m., reservations required. http://www.reservasantaelena.org. (506) 2645-5390.

Selvatura: Self-guided walk on hanging bridges and trails $30. Open daily 7:00 a.m.–4:00 p.m. http://www.selvatura.com. (506) 2645-5929.

Serpentarium (Serpentario): Admission $13. Open daily 9:00 a.m.–8:00 p.m. Guided tours every hour at no additional cost. (506) 2645-6002.

Sky Adventures: Sky Walk hanging bridges, guided tour

only (3 hrs.) $35, daily at 7:30 a.m., 9:30 a.m., 11:30 a.m., 1:30 p.m., and 5:30 p.m. (night tour). Sky Tram gondola ride (1 hr.) $44, daily at 7:30 a.m., 9:30 a.m., 11:30 a.m., and 1:30 p.m. Combination packages available. http://www.skyadventures.travel. (506) 2479-4100 or (506) 2479-4102.

Zip-Line Tour: Several operators in Monteverde/Santa Elena offer tours. A basic canopy tour (2.5-3.5 hrs.) costs $40-70. Tours differ as to what is included (e.g., Superman line, tram ride, Tarzan swing) so be sure to inquire.

Nosara

Horseback Riding: Several operators in Nosara offer beach- and jungle-riding tours. Prices range from $40 (1 hr.) to $55 (2.5 hrs.).

Kayak or Stand-up Paddleboard (SUP) Tour: A few companies in Nosara offer kayak and SUP tours up the Nosara and Montaña Rivers. Kayak tour: $40-65 (2-3 hrs.). SUP tour: $65 (3 hrs.). Kayak rentals also available, 2 hrs., $20 for single kayak or $30 for double kayak.

Refuge for Wildlife: Guided tour of facility and interactive discussion (2 hrs.), 9:30 a.m. (schedule of days changes). Advanced reservations required. Minimum $50 donation per person. Visitors must be age 7 or above (recommended 10 plus) and be in-country for at least 3 days prior to visit (to ensure you do not have a cold, which could spread to the monkeys). http://refugeforwildlife.com. (506) 2682-5049 or (506) 8708-2601.

Sibu Sanctuary: Guided nature hike, tree planting, and tour of facility (2 hrs.), 10:30 a.m. Advanced reservations required. Minimum $50 donation per person. Visitors must be in-country for at least 4 days prior to visit (to ensure you do not have a cold, which could spread to the monkeys). http://nosarasibusanctuary.com. (506) 8413-8889 or (506) 8866-4652.

Poás Volcano Area

Catarata del Toro (Bajos del Toro): Self-guided hike to waterfall $10. Open Mon.–Sat. 8:00 a.m.–5:00 p.m. Closed Sundays. http://www.catarata-del-toro.com. (506) 2476-0800 or (506) 8399-7476.

Doka Estate (San Luis de Sabanilla de Alajuela): Guided coffee tour (1.5 hrs.) $22. Offered daily at 9:00 a.m., 10:00 a.m., 11:00 a.m., 1:30 p.m., 2:30 p.m., and 3:30 p.m., but no 3:30 p.m. tour on Sat. and Sun. Reservations recommended. http://dokaestate.com. (506) 2449-5152 or (506) 2449-6623 or direct toll free from US & Canada 1-888-9-GO-DOKA.

La Paz Waterfall Gardens (Vara Blanca): Self-guided garden tour $38. Open daily 8:00 a.m.–5:00 p.m. Guided tours available with prior reservations. http://www.waterfallgardens.com. (506) 2482-2720 or from US (954) 727-3997.

Poás Volcano National Park: Admission $15. Open daily, 8:00 a.m.–3:30 p.m.

Puerto Viejo de Sarapiquí Area

La Selva Biological Station: Guided nature walk (3.5 hrs.) $45, daily at 8:00 a.m. and 1:30 p.m. Private bird-watching tour (2 hrs.) $70, daily at 5:45 a.m., reservations required. Bird-watching 101 (full-day workshop) $70, 7 person min., reservations required. http://www.threepaths.co.cr/laselva_activities.shtml. (506) 2524-0607 or from US (919) 684-5774.

Nature Pavilion (La Virgen): Self-guided tour $20. Open daily 7:00 a.m.–5:00 p.m. Bird Photography Session on the pavilion (1.5 hrs.) $20, reservations recommended. Guided bird-watching tour (1.5 hrs.) $30, daily at 6:00 a.m., reservations required. http://sarapiquieco-observatory.com/welcome.

Tirimbina Biological Reserve (La Virgen): Self-guided hike $15. Open daily 7:00 a.m.–5:00 p.m. Guided bird-watching (3 hrs.) $25 shared or $50 private, daily at 6:00 a.m., reservations required. http://www.tirimbina.org. (506) 2761-0333 or (506) 2761-0055.

Puerto Viejo de Talamanca Area

Ara Project (Manzanillo site): Guided tour of Manzanillo Great Green Macaw reintroduction station (2.5 hrs.), minimum $20 donation. Daily at 3:00 p.m., reservations required. http://thearaproject.org/visit. (506) 8971-1436.

ATEC (Talamancan Association of Ecotourism and Conservation): Reservations required for all tours. Kèköldi indigenous territory (BriBri) tour (3.5 hrs.) $36. El Yüe Agroeco women's cooperative medicine plants and farm tour (3 hrs.) $25, overnight with meals and lodging, $65. Yorkin (BriBri) women's artisan group full day cultural tour, $88. Overnight with meals and lodging $108. Caribbean cooking class (2-3 hrs.) $55-65, 2 person minimum. http://www.ateccr.org. (506) 2750-0398.

Caribeans: Guided chocolate forest and processing tour

$26. Mon. at 10:00 a.m., Tues. and Thurs. at 10:00 a.m. and 2:00 p.m., Fri. and Sat. at 2:00 p.m. Private tours available with prior reservations (48 hrs. in advance). http://caribeanscr.com. (506) 8836-8930 or (506) 8341-2034.

Finca La Isla Botanical Garden: Self-guided walk through farm, short demonstration, fruit and refreshment $6. Open Fri.–Mon. 10:00 a.m.–4:00 p.m. (other times by appointment). Guided tour (2.5 hrs.) $12 (3 person min., $30 per tour if smaller). 2750-0046 or 8886-8530.

Gandoca-Manzanillo National Wildlife Refuge (Manzanillo): Free and open to the public. Open daily 8:00 a.m.–4:00 p.m.

Jaguar Rescue Center: Guided tour (1.5 hrs.) $18. Mon.–Sat. at 9:30 a.m. and 11:30 a.m. Private tours (2-3 hrs.) $50. Mon.–Sat. at 2:00 p.m., 2 person min., reservations required. http://www.jaguarrescue.com. (506) 2750-0710.

Punta Islita

Ara Project (Punta Islita site): Guided tour of Punta Islita macaw breeding center and reintroduction station (2.5 hrs.), minimum $20 donation. Daily at 3:00 p.m., reservations required. http://thearaproject.org/visit. (506) 6052-9331.

Museo Islita: Free. Open daily 9:00 a.m.–3:00 p.m. (506) 2656-2039.

Sámara

Isla Chora: Several operators in Sámara offer kayak or

stand-up paddleboard tours. Prices range from $35-65 (3 hrs.), includes snorkel gear, water, and a snack. Note that tours usually leave at low tide.

Sámara Trails: Guided hike in Werner-Sauter Biological Reserve (3-3.5 hrs.) $35, daily at 7:00 a.m. and 3:00 p.m. 2 person min., reservations required. http:// samaratrails.com. (506) 8835-9040.

San Gerardo de Dota

Los Quetzales National Park: Admission $10. Open daily, 7:30 a.m.–3:30 p.m.

Tamarindo, Flamingo, and Playa Grande

Marino Las Baulas National Park: Admission $12. Open daily 6:00 a.m.–6:00 p.m. Entrance after dark for turtle viewing must be with a registered guide.

Tamarindo Estuary: Several operators in Tamarindo and Playa Grande offer kayak and boat tours, or you can inquire directly with one of the boats that offer taxi service along the river's edge. Prices range from $35-65 (2-3 hrs.), typically includes light refreshments. Departure times vary depending on the tide.

Tortuguero

Sea Turtle Conservancy Center: Open daily 10:00 a.m.– 12:00 p.m. and 2:00 p.m.–5:30 p.m. (Sun. until 5:00 p.m.). $2 min. donation. http://www.conserveturtles.org.

Tortuguero National Park: Admission $15. Open daily,

6:00 a.m.–4:00 p.m. Beach access available at night with a guide. Turtle-watching tours, around $20 per person. Be sure to hire a registered tour guide.

Turrialba Area

CATIE (Centro Agronómico Tropical de Investigación y Enseñanza): Self-guided tour $10, 7:00 a.m.–4:00 p.m. Guided tours (2 hrs.) also available $25, reservations required. http://www.catie.ac.cr/en/products-and-services/catienatura. (506) 2556-2700.

Guayabo National Monument: Self-guided tour $6. Open daily 8:00 a.m.–3:30 p.m. Guided tours available (1.5 hrs.), starting at additional $5 per person. Reservation with local association of guides is recommended. http://www.usurecr.org. (506) 8534-1063.

Irazú Volcano National Park (near Cartago): Admission $15. Open daily 8:00 a.m.–3:30 p.m.

La Finca Florita (Santa Cruz de Turrialba): Artisanal cheese production tour $30 (1-2 people), $34 (3 people), $40 (4-5 people), and an additional $8 per person after 5. Reservations required. fincalaflorita@hotmail.com. (506) 8624-9682.

Paintball Extremo Turrialba: Open daily 7:30 a.m.–12:00 p.m. (506) 8525-9505.

Paragliding with Parapente Turrialba: Tandem paraglide with guide (15-20 min. flight) $70. Available daily with reservations. http://www.parapenteturrialba.net. (506) 6034-9433.

Parque Paraíso de Volcanes: Available activities include canopy, rappel, ropes course, Tarzan swing, and Superman zip line. Packages start at $50 (4 activities). Open Tues.–Sun., 8:30 a.m.–4:30 p.m. Reservations required at least 24 hrs. in advance. http://www.adventureparaisodevolcanes.com. (506) 2534-0272 or (506) 8729-7247.

Turrialba Volcano National Park: Admission $12. Closed to the public at the time of this writing due to volcanic activity. Visits may be available with a certified guide in the future.

White-Water Rafting: Turrialba has several local rafting companies to choose from. Prices for tours on the Pacuare River range from $80-100 (4 hrs.), includes transportation and lunch. Prices for tours on the Pejibaye River range from $75-85 (2-3 hrs.), includes transportation and a snack.

INDEX

Made in the USA
San Bernardino, CA
06 August 2016